The Spiritual Truth About

Curses
and
Spells

HS Press

THE SPIRITUAL TRUTH ABOUT

CURSES
AND
SPELLS

HOW TO GET OUT OF AN UNHAPPY LIFE

RYUHO OKAWA

HS PRESS

Contents

CHAPTER TWO

Ego, Self, and Self-Reflection
Overcoming suffering from greed

Afterword 117

Preface

This is a simple theme for a religion. However, it seems that as society became more convenient, people became less aware of what a curse is.

Curses already manifest at school during entrance exams, romantic relationships, and also in terms of how you and others perceive and treat you.

When becoming adults, people may be part of a political movement talking about "economic inequality" or saying things such as "Neoliberalism is wrong," "Tax the rich more," or "Give cash handouts and execute Modern Monetary Theory." Such kinds of political measures are out in the world, and the modern curse surely exists in them already.

The manifestation of communism, in itself, is a curse. Also, the Massmedia-democracy that is thought to inhabit one corner of liberalism is filled with curses. You can understand this fully just by looking at newspaper advertisements. I would like for you to learn earnestly about the religious truth that is working behind the scene of curses through this book.

Ryuho Okawa
Master & CEO of Happy Science Group
August 23, 2022

CHAPTER ONE

The Spiritual Truth About Curses and Spells

How to protect yourself from disasters and misfortunes

Originally recorded in Japanese on January 28, 2022
at the Special Lecture Hall of Happy Science in Japan
and later translated into English.

1

The Reality of Curses
That Also Exist Today

Is jealousy a curse?

The title of this chapter might not sound like an everyday matter, but there are many things I want to talk about on this topic. I don't want to make things too difficult, so in this chapter, I would like to give you an overall idea about it.

My books like *Noroigaeshi no Tatakaikata* (lit. "How to Fight Against Curses and Spells") and *Ikiryo-ron* (lit. "About Ikiryo [living ghosts]") are already out, so I think those are helping some people.

I'm not sure whether it is good or bad, but *oni* (ogres in Japanese folklore) is trending in Japan, and there are manga and anime about them too.

The trend before that was *youkai* (monstrous creatures). There was the anime, *Youkai Watch*, and other things about youkai; maybe *Pokémon* is also one of them, although I don't know much about it.

Oni, youkai, and also ikiryo are often seen in TV series. Curses and spells are often covered too.

Actually last night, I watched the rough cut version of the Happy Science movie *The Divine Protector—Master Salt Begins* (executive producer and original story by Ryuho Okawa, concept by Shio Okawa). The filming itself finished in November or December last year (2021), and it is scheduled to be released in fall this year (2022). I watched the first edited version of the movie, which was roughly edited and compressed into two hours.

In the movie, the songs I composed were included, but the soundtracks were not added yet, and the computer graphics were not used at all, so much more work is still needed, which will take more than half a year.

Since I was told that the movie was going to arrive last night, as a preparation, I went to watch an animation movie during the day called *Jujutsu Kaisen* (lit. "Sorcery Fight") *0: The Movie* that is in theaters now (at the time of the lecture).

This series has been published as manga, aired on TV, and made into a movie. However, even when you watch or read them, you can't clearly understand curses or spells. In the movie, it looked like the youkai were simply at war. Many deformed and peculiar creatures appeared, and they vigorously fought against each other to see who was stronger, so it was difficult to see how that was related to curses.

As for our movie, it portrays the practice of repelling curses and spells so it includes a considerable amount of Happy Science teachings. The protagonist, Master Salt, is a super psychic with extraordinary abilities who uses various special curse-repelling rituals to return curses caused by spiritual influences. This is what the movie is mainly about, so I believe you can learn something from here.

Still, there are various people; those who don't understand much about curses, those who can "feel" the curses because such a subculture is spreading, and those who are very curious to know more about curses.

I've heard that non-believers and non-members of Happy Science sometimes come to our staff asking for books related to curses as they feel they are under one. I presume the books that are usually sent to them are the aforementioned *Noroigaeshi no Tatakaikata* and *Ikiryo-ron*.

Curses are a difficult matter to grasp; it is very difficult. On TV, however, I saw an interview with an old man from Kochi prefecture who claimed to be a yin-yang master. What he simply said was, "Well, it's basically jealousy. Curses are just jealousy." By hearing that I thought "Oh, he knows very well."

It is difficult to understand curses when technical terms are used, but put simply, that is it.

As we live in society, some people become superior to others, and a disparity arises. And I'm sure many people have experiences of not being able to achieve their ideal and finding someone else in their desired position or finding someone else possessing what they wanted to have. And the old man I mentioned earlier was saying that feelings like jealousy over those matters are the essence and the main cause of curses. I was impressed by this because it shows that when you are an expert, to some extent, you can give clear answers. Such things do happen.

This world is a competitive society. Since the word *competition* is not so good to use these days, *social inequality* is often used instead. People get those feelings because they want to be equal to and go further than those accomplished individuals. Many people think that a verdict will only be made against them if they act on those feelings, and they will go unnoticed if they only remain as thoughts.

People may have thoughts like, "What's wrong with *just thinking* about it?" "Obviously, people will envy you if you get such good scores, go to such a prestigious school, have such good looks or are born into that good of a family." They believe that just thinking about it in your mind is not a sin, but if you are practicing faith, you will understand that thoughts and actions are truly the same. You will clearly feel or hear them as if you are on a phone call.

If you, for example, send a text message from your phone saying "die, die, die, die," then you would be leaving physical evidence and be charged with blackmail. But if those thoughts are not recorded and remain only in your mind, then, that is not enough for the police to take action in this world.

Thoughts, however, are actually at work and how they work depends on the person you are interacting with. At times your thoughts may have strong and clear effects, while at other times, they won't be as effective and would be repelled.

I said jealousy but actually, *greed*, *anger*, *foolishness*, *pride*, *doubt*, and *false views* are all origin of curses. All of the *six worldly delusions* are related, but jealousy is often the main cause.

First, there is a feeling of jealousy when you compare yourself with other people. That in itself is not a curse, but if it develops—for example, from "I'm so jealous," to "I hate them," or more extreme thoughts such as "I hope they get out of my sight" or "I hope they die"—then you have already set foot into the world of curses or spells.

Curses have the power to bring physical disorder

The scary thing about curses is that when you are actually cursed, sometimes, your hair can start falling out and you can get bald patches, which I have seen happen before. I even made a ritual prayer to deal with it. You really do lose your hair.

In the case of women, I'm sure they'd worry about the future if they get bald patches as a result of other women's jealousy. They may be very scared of becoming like *Oiwa* (a female character from a story whose face became deformed and who has a bald patch on her head). Even just counting the cases that I know, there are several of them, so it can be very scary.

Also, there are times when children lose their hair, but in this case, it is not caused by jealousy among children. When adults start having their own families and children, they can sometimes become jealous of their children. They are adults but still have a child-like mind. When they are sending out thoughts like "I want to be spoiled too" or "I want to be treasured by people around me," even children can experience hair loss, so such a physical phenomenon does happen.

In our movie coming out this fall, you will see a hand-shaped curse mark on someone's neck. It is a true story that actually occurred here (Special Lecture Hall) during a lecture. I'm sure the people who were listening to the lecture in the Special Lecture Hall know, but at that time, a person listening to the talk truly collapsed sideways and was carried out into the hallway. I couldn't say a word about it since I was in the middle of giving the lecture, but the person was sensibly carried out.

When about two people—who were not in the room—saw the handprint on the person's neck, they said, "Isn't this so-and-so's ikiryo?" Then, in response to that, the handprint suddenly vanished.

When you are in Happy Science Religious Affairs Headquarters, everyone is more or less spiritually sensitive, so they can identify the ikiryo just by seeing its handprint. The moment its identity was revealed, the mark disappeared, meaning that once you are caught, that's it. The ikiryo probably thought, "If I get caught, I will be scolded by Master later, so I should leave before that."

This incident is used as one of the plots in the movie. This is a true story, so when the movie gets released, please watch it carefully.

There are also many other cases of physical ailments. In *Ikiryo-ron*, I've talked about my experiences of when I couldn't raise my arm when it became painful or when I couldn't bend my finger. I don't experience them now, but a male executive of Religious Affairs Headquarters is experiencing various things and saying, "For some reason, I feel a piercing pain in my left shoulder" and that he's in pain here and there. I presume he is being "attacked." But since they are not going away, they're not easy opponents.

Based on what I have been seeing in recent years, when unusual things happen to your body, in most cases, problems on the left side indicate that female spirits or thoughts are affecting you, and the right side means male spirits or thoughts are affecting you, and sometimes there can be worse cases.

In this way, many cases of illnesses are sometimes caused by the strong thoughts of someone, or the combined entity of their guardian spirit and their surface consciousness that is affecting you. That is purely ikiryo, but just as it was portrayed in *Jujutsu Kaisen*, sometimes dead spirits may join in as reinforcement. If the living person has similar feelings as the dead spirit, both the ikiryo and the dead spirit sometimes come together; this is a tough case.

We, Happy Science, have had experience in this area for a long time, so sometimes even more "powerful beings" come along, which include various youkai or spirits of foxes that reside in what we call the rear heaven. Foxes also have different levels of spiritual power depending on how many tails—from one to nine—they have. Sometimes it's the fox types and sometimes it's the *tengu* (long-nosed goblins), but there are cases of various youkai, *sennin* (hermits), tengu, and oni coming to you.

Even for oni, there are different kinds. The ones we are using act as the right-hand man of Enma, the King of Judgment in Hell. They are equivalent to prosecutors or the police that punish those who have done evil.

Other oni are like murderers that ate people or killed many people; they are in another type of hell, and they continue doing the same thing. There are murderer-like oni that did bad things like the ones from the island *Onigashima* in an old Japanese folktale; those that commit piracy, looting, arson, murder or thefts. On the other hand, there are oni who can actually become regular light of angels, but instead are working to make sinful people self-reflect in hell.

These kinds of things are not clearly portrayed in manga series like *Demon Slayer: Kimetsu No Yaiba*. They see oni as something different from humans.

In the series, there is the *hashira* (the highest-ranking combatants) of the demon slayer corps who are fighting against the demons, but the red oni and blue oni that we are talking about are like that hashira.

Both sides seem to be of the same kind since they fight in the style of boxing, kicking, judo, karate and kung fu. The difference is that one side has a sense of justice or a specific role, and the others are those who are being chased after.

Those topics are trending at the moment, so they can be a hopeful source to inform people about the Spirit World, and also, some may become more concerned or interested in it.

When looking at various entertainment, I sometimes think that, since I've been doing what I do for decades, quite a lot of my books are being read. In that sense, if I am the "original source" of them, I feel there are many things that I must mention.

2

Adjusting the Jealous Mind—
a Tough Thing to Do
in a Competitive Society

How to adjust your jealous mind that is
sometimes the cause of curses

Now, I will talk about curses.

One thing is that as people live, they can get jealous of others. Although jealousy is a common emotion, there is a degree to how much of it is acceptable.

There is a saying by Konosuke Matsushita, "Jealousy is just right when it is fried golden brown." Jealousy is not a bad thing if it stops at the stage of being "golden brown," but if it reaches the point that it gets "burned black," our mind will turn into hell just as the food becomes harmful and inedible when burnt.

A touch of jealousy can sometimes motivate you to put in greater efforts in competitions, climb the career ladder, study harder or be more attractive. So sometimes, those feelings can be leveraged in a good way. But what would happen if you go to the extreme and it becomes "burnt black"? Even foxes won't eat deep-fried tofu that's burnt and you can't make *inari sushi* (deep-fried tofu filled with sushi rice) with it either. Adjusting this feeling of jealousy is very difficult.

I have been giving talks about how I struggled with controlling my jealousy as the starting point of enlightenment. Still, I sometimes think that the younger people who have joined Happy Science do not know much about this teaching, so it is difficult to get this teaching across or to have them understand it.

Even if they get jealous, they might think that it is a natural human emotion.

It is true that jealousy from a person of a similar level as you may play the role of making you a little humble or keeping your self-assertion in check. The idea behind the mass media or journalism is often founded on jealousy, so if such an emotion becomes prohibited, then they will lose their jobs and people will be disappointed. When prominent or privileged people who are envied by others are attacked for their weaknesses or failures, some people may be relieved or feel that their built-up emotions have been cleared.

If it wasn't through the weekly magazines, people today would write hate comments and spread them online. On a different scale, people in the old days would have stalked or sent threat letters.

It is very difficult to know how much jealousy is acceptable in society. Yet, if those feelings are all dismissed, then we would be left with a world without competition.

The battle against curses seen in competition between professionals

Currently, there've been talks about narrowing the gap of inequality, and it does come with some benefits, but if you are not careful, your advocacy could be jealousy, and that would be exactly the same as Marxism.

But that's only a natural course. Let's say that someone who personally earns and saves ¥1 trillion ($7.3 billion) is considered outrageous when the average saving of the nation is around ¥10 million (about $73,000). Then, if over ¥900 billion was confiscated from that person to dole out, politicians will temporarily gain popularity and seem like they established equality. But that person must have worked incredibly hard to save ¥1 trillion, so if you have a society that completely disregards such things, then everyone will be waiting for pennies from heaven; that is not the kind of society we want.

But before you are able to earn such kind of money, there is a preliminary stage. One is to get good grades at school, enter a good university, then take the road to success, and you will be given status and high income. That is the orthodox way. The same applies if you have outstanding records in sports.

If you win in *Koshien* (high school baseball tournaments) or even if you don't but you are the top pitcher, batter or catcher, you may receive contract money from a professional baseball team worth hundreds of millions of yen and get a high income if all things go well. Such kinds of things happen too, so of course, you will be a target of jealousy from others.

However, it depends on who you become jealous of.

For example, in professional baseball, a Japanese player, Shohei Otani was competing for the top rank in home runs in the 2021 Major League Baseball season. Not only that, but he was also climbing up the ranking of pitcher's winning percentage. It is very rare for one player to take on two roles—being both an ace pitcher and a top-class batter, and people were saying that this has never been done since Babe Ruth. He has a very high income too, but such a person also exists. Ordinary players may be jealous of him, but because he has great force and aura, usually those thoughts are repelled away, and in turn, it often makes those players feel depressed or perform even worse.

In terms of *shogi* (Japanese chess), sometimes the strongest and the top-ranked player is someone who is as young as around 20. Of course, he too had a teacher who trained him—who was at 8-dan—but the fact that he surpassed the teacher and became a champion in various matches shows that the shogi world is also quite a tough one. In fact, a large number of people are probably jealous of him.

I'm sure people are praising him too, but in most cases, such people are shogi fans, and they are not related to the competition itself. People who can see the entire picture will praise him for livening up the shogi world, but I'm sure it's not easy for other professional shogi players to give praise. Some may, in fact, be cursing the person with thoughts like "I hope he dies soon," "His success will be short-lived," or "By the time he reaches 25, he'll be no good." So, he must repel these thoughts away.

Sota Fujii has also won numerous crowns, and he is currently battling for the 5th crown, so I don't know the results (at the time of the lecture. He currently holds 5 crowns). He was saying that when he has a big match coming, he watches Bruce Lee's movie, *Enter the Dragon* on repeat as if to imprint victory into his mind.

In the movie, you see Bruce fight shouting "Ackchooww!" so I wondered, "Interesting, shogi with *Enter the Dragon*. Is it OK to be that energized?" It may be that you need a martial arts-like spirit and be prepared to fight like Bruce Lee, since the opponent will also engage in the match with extremely strong willpower. As you get stronger, more enemies will arise, and if they are all wishing for your loss, then maybe such preparation is necessary.

Usually, if there is a huge gap in strength between yourself and the opponent, even if you curse them, it will be repelled back to yourself. Unfortunately, it gets shot back at you and its content will return to you, so it has no effect. However, when it is between rivals, the curse may work on both sides.

Even if players are competing, they would still have compassion for the other person. At times, they may receive various information like when the opponent loses this match, he will fall off a rank—from class A to B, from B to C, or that if he loses this match, he will be divorcing.

Having to hear such things are also quite tough. It is hard to go on living in such a way, but since winning is their job, they cannot avoid competing. This is reality.

3

"Short-Distance Runner"-Like Thinking Can Lead to Curses

A crime caused by a student who was too immersed in a short span competition

In recent cases, there were two incidents regarding the entrance exam.

One was an incident caused by a high school student from Nagoya aspiring to get into the University of Tokyo, Natural Sciences III (faculty which leads to the Faculty of Medicine). He was only 17, so his name and face were not disclosed, but apparently his family reported him missing to the police after he left home feeling very irritated because his grades got worse. He traveled to Tokyo and came to the gate of the University of Tokyo and stabbed two students—who were there for exams—and an old man. On top of that, he brought petrol and set fire to a couple of places; he claimed that he also wanted to die.

Looking at this incident, not all people who took the exam there were applying for Natural Sciences III at the University of Tokyo (the university was one of the venues of entrance exams for all national universities). The people who were stabbed were completely unrelated to his rage, so it is truly saddening. He stabbed people from Chiba Prefecture, and the old man was completely unrelated too.

I understand that he was irritated, but even if he was in the smart class to get into the top class of the University of Tokyo, if he stabbed people, then of course he could not stay in school and will be expelled. And that means he cannot enter university either. I simply wonder why such a polar opposite thing happened when he must have known about its consequences.

Even a high school student from a more rural place who reads the local newspaper would know how problematic it would be and that it would even ruin his future. Even if you don't read the newspaper, if you just glance at the occasional newspaper ads for weekly magazines, you can predict its consequences. These kinds of things are not part of the academic curriculum for the exam. People who have properly studied constitutional and criminal law understand the kind of prosecution they will have to face, but those who haven't studied it won't know about it. That is why they become emotional and act in desperation and do whatever. This, in a way, is indeed a "curse" and it is unfortunate for the victims who got caught up in it.

There are hundreds of thousands of students who are taking entrance exams, but the reality is that even if people try to, many people cannot get into the University of Tokyo, Natural Sciences III, so they give up. The majority of the people are not at the level to even think about applying in the first place, so the fact that you are smart enough to want to apply means you are one of the quite capable people. That alone is impressive. Many people give up that path, and there are various other universities, so you can look for the ones you can actually get into.

It doesn't have to be the University of Tokyo. There is medicine at Nagoya University, Osaka University, Kyushu University, and other national and private universities too. If you don't have money, there are also scholarships. When you look into it, you can pick from these choices.

Some people apply to the Faculty of Medicine at the University of Tokyo just to prove they are intelligent, but many are actually not fit to become doctors. It seems that many of those who passed would faint at the sight of blood. Even if they are good at English and mathematics and they become doctors, many people are actually not suited for the job.

I don't know about it now but during my days, the average pass rate of the national examination for doctors was 80% in Japan. And even those from medicine at the University of Tokyo, out of the 100 students that applied for the examination, about 90 passed and 10 failed.

There are many people who don't feel motivated even after getting into the university since they aren't suitable to become doctors. As some students work as tutors, they go astray from the doctors' path and end up becoming cram school teachers. There are others who take up a different road too. That is why the pass rate of the national examination in most cases would only reach around 90%, despite getting into the Natural Sciences III.

On the other hand, more medical students from Keio University pass the examination. Nada High School, a prestigious all-boys school in Hyogo Prefecture has their students apply for both Keio and the University of Tokyo, and by looking at how many have gotten accepted to medicine at Keio, they predict how many will get into the Natural Sciences III at the University of Tokyo. When it comes to Keio medical students for example, the pass rate of examination for doctors is about 99%. I guess since Keio is expensive, students certainly try and recover the cost. It has always been the case that more students in national universities go out and have fun since tuition is cheap, but Keio (a private university) has kept its pass rate at 99%.

For example, the faculty of medicine at Tokushima University or much lower regional universities—although I won't say the name of them because I might get punished—have a 100% pass rate.

The fact that the pass rate is 100%—100 people applying and 100 people passing—means it is above the University of Tokyo or Keio. Although it is more difficult to get into those places, students from regional universities happen to entirely pass the national examination for doctors.

All of them take the same exam, but the result depends on how each of them tackles it.

It is true that even if you enter the faculty of medicine at Tokushima University, unless you work with the utmost effort and pass the national examination for doctors, it doesn't mean anything in a rural area. So, I presume they are working extremely hard.

Well, some of the private universities with a low pass rate are like 60%, so it must be tough for them too.

These are also some of the cases, so it is quite sad that they burn out from competing too much in such a short span.

Passing examinations is not everything —there is no end to developing yourself

Another incident on the news was of a girl who hid her phone in her sleeve during a public examination, took photos of the questions from world history, and sent them to four students. They were students from the University of Tokyo looking to be hired as an online tutor. The girl sent the photos to them, telling them that she was giving them a test of ability to see who she would hire and had them answer the questions. Without knowing this, two of them gave the answers.

There have been many ways of cheating since the old days. It started with things like opening up a pencil and hiding a cheat sheet inside and escalated to cheating in the restroom. Even in a shogi match, in the past, someone was suspected of using a laptop to go through old shogi matches and look for good moves in the restroom or somewhere, because he left his seat for one or two hours to think about the next move.

In any case, it is not good to cheat. Eventually, you will have to face the worst consequences.

Therefore, although I understand people becoming jealous of others with good grades or who pass the exam, the only way to deal with such things is to accept the fact as it is.

Strangely, it is more common for those who are good at studying and are intelligent to have an inferiority complex and be easily hurt. They are bothered by the smallest difference in grades. It is quite common for people who were doing very well in middle school to become average in high school. Smart people will go to schools with such intelligent people, and there are various cases like smart students in primary school becoming average in junior high school, smart students in junior high school becoming average in high school, or smart students in high school becoming below average at universities. It is in fact very strange, but that is how things are.

If that person is working hard to just get into the school as if sprinting a short-distance race, what I commonly hear is that they burn out after they finish the exam. I have seen many people who have fallen greatly, so it is important that you live your life with both a short-distance runner and a long-distance runner mentality.

Controlling jealousy is a very important matter when you are studying for exams as well.

In sports, some people pull out when they see obvious differences in talent between them and other players. For the things related to strength, 80% of it is possibly determined at birth. To become a professional in sports, having good genetics regarding physical strength helps to some extent, but of course you must work hard.

Additionally, it may depend on what sport it is.

For example, it is said that judo is 70% strength and 30% technique, but kendo is 30% strength and 70% technique. Kendo uses a bamboo sword so what that means is that a person can become strong at it if they practice. Since using something is different from wrestling with bare hands, when you have technique, you can in fact be strong even if you have a small build or are old.

Kendo teachers with a high rank will still be strong even in their 60s, 70s or 80s. That is because they use a bamboo sword. Of course, I'm sure that younger people with more strength will be stronger at physical fighting. For things like judo, your own strength will play a big role.

In this way, things may differ depending on which sports you are playing.

But to go as far as becoming a professional tennis player who earns billions of yen (tens of millions of dollars), one must have a body fit to be an athlete, be gifted physically, and have gone through rigorous training since a young age; maybe they were lucky with coaches too. Apparently, there is something like an elite course or study abroad program in sports.

Considering such things, young people have to partake in numerous competitions and I'm sure they sometimes envy others. I myself experienced it a lot when I was young.

As you become more successful and enter places such as schools or workplaces that are highly respected, or jobs that require qualifications, you begin to be mediocre in that field. You gradually become like an average person.

Even if you pass the bar examination and become a lawyer, some will keep winning and others will always lose in court. The winning percentage indeed varies from person to person. Even if you pass the same exam, it happens.

I believe it has become easier to be lawyers now since law schools have been introduced, but in my days, not even one in 60 people could pass the bar exam, so on average, people took the exam nine times before passing. They usually pass the exam before turning 30 years old—so between 29 to 30—but the time spent on their studies is like you are attending cram school and you are basically living a life of a jobless person.

On average, those people live like that for nine to ten years so it is quite normal to start feeling mentally unstable. You won't gain any new social knowledge just by memorizing the laws, reading the same books, and studying the same kind of workbooks every year.

In actual fact, even if you work in a legal profession, at times you may lose the case for not knowing about events happening throughout society and the world. There are many things lawyers don't know about, but they will be consulted with many specific problems.

Therefore, it will be troublesome if they don't know about the world.

If you didn't watch TV, read newspapers, watch the news, read manga, watch movies, and didn't do anything but memorize the law textbooks, then actually, you won't be able to give answers during the consultations you have with people.

For example, if a client came and said "I envied a member of Nogizaka46 (a Japanese female idol group) so I stalked her to try and end her career," but if the lawyer didn't know of such an idol group, or any other related groups like AKB48 or only having heard a little about Onyanko Club (a Japanese idol group in the 1980s), then the client will just leave. They will think it's a waste of time and never consult that lawyer again, and that means the lawyer lost a client.

As these things show, passing examinations is not everything, and you also need to study various other matters. That is why, there is no end to developing yourself.

4

Keeping Your Jealousy Under Control

Jealousy can turn people into hellish beings, youkai, oni, and tengu

As I said earlier, I think there is a lot of jealousy in the world. I had heard something like the following: A student who got top grades in his class in Tokyo when he was in junior high school ended up scoring second to last in high school. He then committed suicide by jumping off the station platform and into the oncoming train. Ever since, the school stopped posting the ranks of students who scored in the bottom one-third or one-fourth. Some schools draw a wavy line to omit the grades in the bottom ranks.

When one of my children went to Kaisei Junior & Senior High School, which the current prime minister used to attend long ago, they printed and distributed the scores of the first place student all the way down to the hundredth place back. Naturally, that fueled fierce competition. When they held a field day, someone set fire to the equipment room in the gymnasium. It means someone had a grudge against someone. So, the school stopped posting the grades.

As you can see, too wide of a gap—such as between the rich and the poor—can lead to criminal acts. So, you should really watch out for grudges and jealousy.

The same goes for a person's face. "Oiwa" might have been a beauty in the past. In a movie, I remember she was depicted as a beautiful teacher of *shamisen* music who fell in love with a young man, but when the man went for a younger woman, she told him she would curse him to death if he ever married the other woman.

It is terrifying beyond imagination to see a beautiful woman turn into a ghost. It isn't as terrifying to see a not-so-beautiful woman turn into an unsightly being, but it's absolutely scary to see a beautiful woman like that.

I would rather not see Hitomi Kuroki, a Japanese actress, playing the role of "Oiwa." I really do not want to see her like that. It's scary.

In this way, you can find countless things to be jealous about if you compare yourself with other people, so you must control your jealousy well. Even if you do not commit a crime in a worldly sense, if you continue to live with an envious mind, you might end up in hell. What is worse, you might curse people even after you've gone to hell.

Perhaps you might curse or possess others because you were killed by them, which is understandable, but you will only make yourself more miserable.

People with an aggressive personality will try to kill others; on the other hand, passive people might fail to commit suicide—or they might commit suicide repeatedly in the other world.

So, a curse is essentially the desire to destroy someone's happiness or to bring misfortune upon someone, and the majority of curses come from jealousy.

It is quite natural for humans to be jealous, but how you control your jealousy is the beginning of "keeping your mind under control." Jealousy can turn you into a hellish being or possibly youkai, oni, or tengu, so please control it well.

Repelling jealousy is one way to deal with it. In some cases, people can repel jealousy by using some kind of sorcery, incantations, or rituals. Another method would be to reflect the jealousy back to the person who emitted it. I will speak more on this at another time.

What if you are cursed by someone with the very strong willpower?

Sometimes, you might be affected by jealousy. Or you could become similar to the one who is jealous of you, or be possessed by an evil spirit. Either way, it won't be a happy thing for you. If you keep your mind well-polished, you can basically return the curse back to the source, but sometimes the other person could have very strong willpower.

Simply put, each person has a different level of strong willpower. So, if someone with very strong willpower is cursing you, you won't be able to repel the curse so easily. You may need to consult a professional, such as a religious expert, a priest of a Shinto shrine or Buddhist temple, or someone with the Dharma power.

In the movie *Jujutsu Kaisen*, there is a technical college called Jujutsu Kosen, which categorizes students into four classes, Grades 1-4, based on their abilities. There might have been a Semi-Grade 1, but anyway, there are roughly four classes.

The main character transfers in his first year of high school as a Special Grade. He has the abilities of a Special Grade.

Why is he a Special Grade? I will refrain from giving away spoilers because some people may get annoyed if I did. Anyhow, the main character is a descendant of one of the Three Great Vengeful Spirits. There are four Special Grades, and toward the end of the movie, they fight against the Special Grade vengeful spirits.

The point is, there are different levels to curses. So, if you curse someone more powerful than you, you may be defeated.

When my uncle passed away long ago, I did not attend his funeral because I was busy, but I wondered why his spirit didn't come to me. Usually, someone close to me would come after they died. Years after his death, I asked his spirit and he said, "There were Tokyo Dome-like layers of the dome, and I couldn't see you. So, I didn't know how to reach you or get near you. I can come to you if you call me, but I can't see you." I guess that is the work of the staff of Religious Affairs Headquarters and Happy Science as a whole.

However, a person inside the dome would be able to "throw a ball" and hit me, so it's likely that they will become ikiryo. It is quite a difficult matter. Some of my disciples compete with each other or grow jealous of each other. If they turn into ikiryo, then sadly, they expose all their attachments to common worldly desires such as status, money, opposite sex, and fame, which are all things they are required to control by undergoing spiritual discipline.

They can try hard to keep their thoughts from showing up on the surface, but their ikiryo will be much more straightforward. So, I guess the only way to make them understandable for people in manga or anime is to depict them as monsters.

5

Keeping Away from Jealousy

Mr. Shoichi Watanabe's eye-opening words

Basically, curses come from jealousy. Now, how can you keep yourself away from it? I have taught you about it many times before. I, also, used to suffer from it in my younger days, and I remember reading the following in a book written by Mr. Shoichi Watanabe.

Mr. Watanabe also suffered a lot in his younger days. He was raised in Yamagata Prefecture, a countryside, so he was not very blessed in terms of his learning environment; he had less information compared with the academic elites in the major cities. Also, although his family was fairly wealthy before he went to university, as soon as he did, his father failed in his investments and the family went bankrupt. So, he had no choice but to do his absolute best in his studies and get top scores, because only the top student had their tuition waived. Otherwise, he could not graduate.

Mr. Watanabe said he had a tough time fighting back his resentment toward the students who were rich or who got excellent grades. He also said that, in the Christian context, the opposite of jealousy is not love but congratulating others. It means to say something good about the other person. He realized this important truth.

It is a very important point. I, also, realized this and scales fell from my eyes. Mr. Watanabe wrote about such an experience in his book, *Quality Life no Hasso* (lit. "Thinking of a Quality Life") which might be found only as second-hand books now.

In the end, you must learn that being jealous or envious of others will not make things better for you.

Japanese people have a very strong tendency to seek equality, so they dislike those who are outstanding and want to shut them out, but won't complain as long as everyone is the same. This is said to be due to their long history as an agricultural society. Farming or agriculture depends a lot on the climate and cannot be done by human effort alone. So, Japanese people seek an equal society. They naturally have a strong sense of jealousy toward successful people, but will be kind to those who are the same as them.

People of Japanese descent overseas have a similar trait. Descendants of Japanese immigrants in Hawaii have a strong tendency to seek equality and harbor jealousy; they are apt to drag people who grow very rich or become successful.

It reminds me of the "crabs in a bucket" mentality. When a crab tries to climb out of a bucket, other crabs grab onto it and drag it down. When another one climbs up, it is also dragged down. In this way, the crabs pull each other down, one by one, so none of them are able to get out of the bucket.

If a crab can get to the rim of the bucket, pull the next one up before going down to the other side, and have others follow his example, then they can all get out, but they prevent themselves from getting out by dragging down any crab that tries to go up.

It is very similar to the story, *The Spider's Thread* by Ryunosuke Akutagawa. It goes like this: Shakyamuni Buddha was taking a stroll around the lotus pond. He looks through the pond and sees hell, where spirits of the dead are suffering in agony in the Hell of the Bloody Pond. Among them was a man drowning—his name was Kandata.

Buddha thought, "When Kandata was alive, he didn't do any good deeds—except, he once saved a spider's life. As he was walking, he came across a spider and almost stepped on it, but instead saved its life. He did one good deed, so I'll give him a chance." Buddha then lowered a spider's thread down into the pond.

On seeing the thread come down, Kandata grasped it tightly. You might think that the spider's thread would snap, but surprisingly, it was quite strong like Spider-Man's thread. Kandata climbed up the thread. When he was climbing up, he looked down and saw others also coming up the thread. He told them, "This is *my* thread. All of you, let go of it!" He had no virtue. He only thought of saving himself.

Then, the thread snapped and he fell back into the Hell of the Bloody Pond. That is the whole story. It ends with something like, "It was almost noon in Paradise. Shakyamuni Buddha was walking around quietly."

Happy Science has published a picture book of this story called *Miracle Soncho no Ohanashi: Kumo no Ito* (lit. "Elder Miracle's Story: The Spider's Thread"). Anyway, the story is about jealousy, just like the analogy of the crabs in a bucket I mentioned earlier. If you wish to only save yourself or only benefit yourself, you might become like the student I talked about in Section 3 who turned into a criminal.

Would a sumo wrestler be jealous of a tennis player?

The person you become jealous of is, in the psychological sense, someone you want to be like the most. You won't be jealous of someone who you don't want to be like. So, you should first know that people grow jealous of what is their interests and concern.

For example, someone aiming to become a sumo wrestler would be jealous and think it's unfair for another sumo wrestler to win his third championship, bearing ill feelings toward him becoming an *ozeki* (champion). But many people in the world have a 0% chance of becoming a sumo wrestler; over 99% of them have no chance. To those people, it's not a big deal for a sumo wrestler to win three championships and become an ozeki. They would learn about it on the news and think, "Oh, is that so." But of course, the people who want to become professional sumo wrestlers might harbor jealousy toward the champion.

Then, would a sumo wrestler be jealous of the world champion in tennis? Probably not. In sumo, it's better for a *yokozuna* (grand champion) to be heavier, larger, and taller. And, he would need to do *shiko* (foot-stomping exercise) and pushing exercises every day. This is absolutely different from the training that a professional tennis player does. So, a sumo wrestler wouldn't want to become a tennis player.

The basic idea in sumo is, "There are gold coins buried in the *dohyo* ring. So, work for your money by fighting on the dohyo." Therefore, people don't grow jealous of others who are different from them.

People working in a field that requires math skills or those who want to get into a school that requires such skills may get jealous of someone who excels in math. On the contrary, it may not matter so much to the people who are working in a field that doesn't require math. So, it's not so simple; it depends on the person.

Oftentimes, officers of the Ministry of Finance are graduates of the Faculty of Law or the Faculty of Economics, but a former officer, now a critic, who was a graduate of the University of Tokyo's Faculty of Science and went to graduate school wrote something like this.

"There were about 20 of us who joined the ministry in the same year, but I didn't see anyone else who graduated with a degree in the sciences. It was just me. So, although I heard them boast about having a degree in law or economics, in my eyes, their 'math skills' were at a primitive level—they were doing arithmetic. On the other hand, I could see all the statistics just by taking a look at the numbers. I thought, 'Are you serious? People with a degree in humanities are dumb.'"

Of course, he would think so. Someone who did well or majored in the sciences would see it that way.

But from the standpoint of someone who graduated in the humanities, namely law, they would probably think, "He does well in math, but knows nothing about the law." So, it applies to both sides. If they are in the same workplace, they might accuse each other of their shortcomings.

6

Congratulating Others Can Bring Changes to Human Relationships

So anyway, I chose to accept the idea of congratulating others. I was about 20 years old at the time.

Many people in the world are more talented than I am. They get better grades, have a special ability in something, are better looking, wear expensive clothes because their family is rich, are popular with girls, or have smooth pick-up lines. I have seen many people like that and was sometimes envious of them.

But as Mr. Shoichi Watanabe said, "Stop being jealous and congratulate others instead. Make efforts to do that," I tried my best to compliment those who got better grades than I did. I made efforts to tell them verbally, "That was amazing," "You did well on this," and "You're very smart." I gave my best to compliment others rather than to get rid of my jealousy.

This period of one or two years was a tough time for me, but strangely enough, the people I congratulated —those who seemed to be quite different from me

—approached me and became friends with me. It was an interesting experience; if you are jealous of them and dislike them, they would stay away, but if you congratulate them, they come and make friends with you.

Most of my friends were often outstanding, unlike me. Quite a few of my university classmates went on to succeed in their careers. Although I didn't know anything specific, they had much better talent than I did and received better grades. And when I praised them, surprisingly, they came to be friends with me. It made me wonder why.

They gave me different kinds of advice, but sadly, some of them ended up doing something illegal and were sent to jail. Yes, it's a mystery.

I was also reading books on other subjects while my friends were studying for a certification exam or a term exam. I couldn't contain my desire to read other books; I couldn't help but read books on cultivating myself or developing my philosophy and just couldn't stick to reading books on law alone, so I tried to be efficient in my studies and to make time to read other books.

Of course, my friends often got better grades because they were only studying for exams, but since I had the heart to congratulate these outstanding people, they stayed close to me. And they were quite successful in their work.

They were successful, but some of them were accused of breaking the law.

One of them became a diplomat. When he was renewing his passport, he called a married woman to come to meet him at the station platform, and he was arrested there. You might not believe this, but it happened. It is true that a diplomat is not an expert on the law. Perhaps it was against international law. He had trouble renewing his passport, so he asked the woman to meet him at the station platform, but instead, a female officer came and arrested him. He worked for the Ministry of Foreign Affairs, but lost his qualification as a diplomat and I haven't heard anything about him since.

Another person I know is Mr. Kurokawa (Hiromu Kurokawa, former chief of the Tokyo High Public Prosecutors Office). Recently, an article in a weekly magazine said that he was appointed the outside director of a company (at the time of this recording). Although we took the same course at university, we weren't so close; we didn't know each other so well.

I took the bar exam later than the people around me. At that time, I heard that Kurokawa was telling people there was no way I would fail; I thought that was nice of him. Although we didn't hang out together, he was saying to other people that I was the last person to fail.

He was a candidate for the next prosecutor-general, which he couldn't become after covering up for Mr. Abe (former Prime Minister Shinzo Abe). His highest position was chief of the Tokyo High Public Prosecutors Office. By the way, the other candidate, who became the prosecutor-general, was also one of my classmates.

So, as I was not jealous of Mr. Kurokawa, he spoke of me in such a way. I was not so good at studying, but he said there was no way I would fail an exam, and I am still thankful for that even though decades have passed.

However, he was fined for mahjong gambling—a game that uses matchsticks as chips—against some journalists, for about ¥20,000 or ¥30,000 ($140 or $210). I feel a little sorry for him.

But it seems that thanks to Mr. Kurokawa, Prime Minister Abe did not have to go to jail. If a different type of person were the prosecutor, Mr. Abe could have gone to jail. Even in my eyes, it's possible to file the case. It's just that Mr. Kurokawa was covering up for Mr. Abe. The vice-minister of justice and other higher-ups were covering up for Mr. Abe, so he couldn't be arrested. The special investigations unit couldn't move, either. So, although Mr. Kurokawa was considered the bad guy, he probably fulfilled his mission.

As for Mr. Abe, obviously, it would cost a lot of money to invite people from Yamaguchi Prefecture to have them stay at a hotel and enjoy the cherry blossom viewing party. If you include travel, accommodation, and food, the total expense would be tremendous, so he would naturally want to compensate for that even just a little. I can understand that, but if he does that for a long time, he will eventually get used to it and lose the feeling that he's doing something wrong. In reality, it is probably the people around him who are taking care of such things.

The longest-serving prime minister, including before and after WWII, was bombarded with questions such as, "Did you compensate for the costs of the cherry blossom viewing party?" "Did you give special consideration to your wife's friend who bought land for a school at a lower price?" Mr. Kurokawa probably did all he could to prevent Mr. Abe's arrest.

It's similar to a *jidaigeki* (a drama based on various periods in Japanese history) when a chief retainer would take the blame and perform *seppuku* (hara-kiri) to protect his lord. So, if Mr. Kurokawa saw value in such a life, then that's fine. It's more political than a simple matter of law.

Also, as written in *The Laws of the Sun*, when my friend who passed the bar exam and became a lawyer heard that I was going to work for a trading company, he repeatedly insisted I should not work there.

He said, "Trading companies are for people who can drink, gamble, and buy. You can't drink alcohol. You can't gamble. You don't play mahjong. You don't buy

The Laws of the Sun
(New York: IRH Press, 2018)

women. You can't possibly work for a trading company when you can't do any of these. Stop, don't do it."

Even as the day of graduation was approaching, he kept telling me, "What a shame. You must take the bar exam again. Something was obviously wrong this year, but it sometimes happens, so take the exam again next year. Don't work for a trading company." He was a good friend. He warned me, and he, himself, was outstanding; he passed the bar exam while he was a student.

But unfortunately, decades later, he embezzled the ¥50 million or ¥60 million ($350 thousand or $420 thousand) he was entrusted with from his client. He was arrested and his law license was revoked. I couldn't believe it. A lawyer was entrusted ¥50 million or ¥60 million yen from his client. If he uses the money for his own benefit, that would be misappropriation, malpractice, or whatever it's called. This is obvious. There was no way he wouldn't know that, so I wondered what had happened to him.

He might have been short on funds and thought, "I'll just borrow the money for now and return it later."

I couldn't believe his downfall due to something like that. So, I was sad.

People who passed the bar exam violated the law and fell from grace. Life is full of ups and downs. They, themselves, are the ones to blame, of course. But if they are caught off guard, they could fall, and sometimes it could be due to a curse.

7

Living a Life Free from Curses

Jealousy from an unexpected person

As I started Happy Science and took part in many activities, I must have become the subject of jealousy from other religious leaders, writers, and so on. But I was quite carefree and did not feel anything.

Mr. Shoichi Watanabe talked about another way to avoid jealousy. "If someone is jealous of you, you should keep doing what they don't like. Then, they will give up and stop being jealous of you. Their jealousy toward you means they want you to stop doing something or they don't want you to become something, so if you keep doing what you do, they will stop being jealous of you."

I, on the other hand, did not notice others being jealous of me. I was just doing my work without worrying about that. But sometimes, an unexpected person could be jealous of you. For example, Akiyuki Nosaka, a writer who won the Naoki Prize (a prestigious

Japanese award for the best work of popular literature), was jealous of me—we recorded a spiritual message from him. He was much older than me and I did not take much notice of him, but he was jealous of me. I had no idea.

In 1991, we had our ad printed in newspapers: "*The Terrifying Revelations of Nostradamus* / 700,000 copies, first printing." We did that because even after all the books we sold and all the lectures we held, the mass media absolutely ignored us. So, we decided to take a more aggressive approach. Then, Mr. Nosaka appeared on TV and gave a hostile comment that I was the second coming of Hitler.

Taking this into account, I gave a lecture for about an hour explaining the difference between Hitler and Christ. After watching a recording of my lecture, he said that I was indeed Hitler. I thought, "Oh, is that how he thinks of me?"

But some time after that, he said he would not criticize me anymore. He wrote something like, "My daughter told me, 'Stop it, Dad. There is no doubt Mr. Okawa is God. You are going against God. If you attack or be jealous of God, you will definitely lose your luck and spend your last days in misery. He is God, so stop it already, Dad.' I wanted to criticize that Hitler-like guy more and bring him down, but I'll stop since my daughter told me to." Later on, he said he might have been jealous of me after all because although he was a Naoki Award winner, he could only publish 7,000 copies on first printing whereas we advertised 700,000 copies, and that really irritated him. His words left an impression on me.

Sometime around then, Mr. Tamio Kageyama, who was a Happy Science member and also a Naoki Prize winner, asked me to have a talk session with him. It was for an article in a magazine. But since I was busy and was not reading many of his books that much, I declined it. I didn't think I could give a good talk session. However, he told me he was glad that I declined it. He said something like, "If I had a talk session with you, I would've gotten full of myself. I would've made a mistake. But since you declined my offer, I was able to follow you as a believer." So, although people can be in similar positions, they can go in different ways.

As a religious leader, I could be receiving a lot of jealousy from many people without realizing it.

Sometimes, I see book titles or ads that make me think people are competing with me, but I try not to think about them. That is why I do not sense jealousy toward myself.

You could send congratulatory thoughts to the people who are jealous of you. But in some cases, you might not know that they are jealous of you. In that case, you should carefully guard yourself and boldly continue to do what you must at the same time.

When you become way beyond their level, they will no longer see any meaning in being jealous of you.

On the other hand, it is not good to worry excessively, either. You might stop applying makeup because someone said, "She's beautiful. Maybe she's good at applying makeup" about you, or you might stop wearing a certain brand because someone said, "She's only beautiful because of her clothes. The brand she's wearing makes her look pretty" about you. I know you might think and act like that to defend yourself, but you shouldn't be too extreme.

If you think what you are doing is right, you should do it. You do not need to lower yourself to their level.

Don't deny your ideals; direct your mind toward heaven

I have given some examples of a curse. Perhaps you feel like you want to curse someone because they hurt you. I can understand that you want to take revenge. But sometimes you might have insulted others without knowing that you did or sometimes, the other person may have felt insulted without you knowing. This is quite difficult, but you should try to avoid insulting or making fun of someone so blatantly.

Long ago, when people were starting to recognize me, I read a newspaper article that said a literature graduate of the University of Tokyo who graduated around the same time as I was writing books and working as a critic. When this person was asked to name a friend during his years at the university, he said, "Ryuho Okawa."

But I did not know him at all. I thought, "Friend? How are we friends if I don't even know him?" And when I said that he was not my friend, he got really angry.

I had no idea who he was, but the article said I was his friend. Maybe he wanted to gain fame by mentioning me but could no longer retract it after saying that to the people around him.

Therefore, someone could be holding a grudge against you without you knowing. Anyway, you shouldn't willfully belittle, mock, or make a fool of someone.

Furthermore, it's not good to flatter, butter up to, or brownnose someone. However, if you honestly feel that the person has good or wonderful points, it would be good to praise and congratulate them. In that way, you can survive without being affected by curses.

Nowadays, ikiryo is a serious problem. The current internet-based society seems like a world of ikiryo in a visible form. Each person can send out and spread all kinds of information, so it's as if they are spreading curses everywhere.

How the human mind should be is basically the same in any age. It's important to direct your mind toward heaven, lead others, and help others. Also, encourage yourself and make efforts to improve yourself in a good way.

Another thing is not to worry too much. If you feel strong jealousy toward someone, please try to remember what I said.

After all, being jealous means you deny your ideal image on the subconscious level, and your subconsciousness accepts that. That is why you cannot be who you want to be.

For example, like all communists, if you are always criticizing rich people, you will never be rich. If you think rich people are bad people and that makes you keep on bad-mouthing them, it will stop you from getting rich.

People who criticize executives won't be able to start their own companies and succeed as an executive. You must know that.

Most of the time, the target of your jealousy is your ideal image, so if you want to be like them, you should make an effort to see their good points and act like them. If they are beyond your reach, you can either accept it and give up, or switch to a "long-distance runner" type of thinking.

In this chapter, I spoke about the overall idea of curses in a general way. Curses are everywhere now, so please be careful. At the same time, our movie this coming fall (*The Divine Protector—Master Salt Begins*) should turn out well, so please look forward to it.

CHAPTER TWO

Ego, Self, and Self-Reflection
Overcoming suffering from greed

Originally recorded in Japanese on January 4, 2018,
at the Special Lecture Hall of Happy Science in Japan,
and later translated into English.

1

Egolessness—Its True Meaning Taught by Buddha

In terms of Buddhist teachings, the topic of this chapter is entry-level and will cover the basics of the basics. Ironically, many people study a lot of difficult things, but they either forget or do not understand the most basic Truth. So, I hope to teach in simple words what Buddha tried to teach or what his essential thinking was.

As studies on Buddhism progressed over the years, their contents became more complicated and technical, just like studies for an entrance examination for school. For this reason, people began to lose sight of the original purpose of Buddhism along the way. So, I believe it is sometimes important to return to the starting point and repeatedly talk about topics on the mind in a way that is easy to understand.

The title of this chapter is "Ego, Self, and Self-Reflection." It'll talk about "Ego and the Self" which are major issues that many Buddhist and religious scholars have failed to understand.

This problem did not start recently; it began more than 2,000 years ago. A little while after Buddha passed away, the Buddhist organization began to divide, and a group of very philosophical-minded people already started getting the wrong understanding of them. Since then, for more than 2,000 years, many have continued to misunderstand them significantly.

Where did they go wrong? As one of the core teachings of Buddhism, there is the word *muga* in Japanese, which literally means "no ego." It means to "let go of ego" or "egoless." I believe the problems concern the understanding of this Buddhist term *muga* or "no ego." In other words, how the disciples and scholars of later generations understood its meaning had changed considerably from what Buddha had originally taught.

Buddha's teaching on *muga* is "Do not be selfish" or "Do not live your life in a self-centered way." In other words, it means, "Don't just live only for your ego." This is what he wanted to say.

In India, the word for self or ego is *atman*, and the word *muga* or "no ego" is derived from *anatman*. By adding "an" to atman, it becomes anatman which literally means "no self." So, *muga* can easily be confused to mean "non-existence of self."

Moreover, since atman can also mean soul or spirit, some people automatically assumed that Buddha denied the existence of the soul because Buddhism taught about anatman also.

In this way, many people started to question and debate whether souls actually exist or not.

The debate still goes on today. To people who haven't come across a soul or haven't had spiritual experiences, such disputes may sound trivial and only concern abstract and theoretical issues. But to those who have had actual spiritual experiences, the existence of the soul is indisputable.

Suppose Shakyamuni Buddha, who founded and established Buddhism 2,500 or 2,600 years ago, taught that "souls do not exist" and this teaching continued to spread for over 2,500 years. Anyone will know how nonsensical this sounds.

If this was true, then this is the same as what anyone today—who has had no spiritual experiences or was not taught about religion from their family—thinks. Schoolteachers, government officials, doctors, and whoever they may be all say, "When we die, that's the end. Humans are just physical bodies. No one has seen souls." Can we say that all these people have already awakened and become modern buddhas? Absolutely not. Such people cannot be called enlightened people.

Considering such people as enlightened ones will be the same as thinking that a primitive person, who lived 2,500 or 2,600 years ago, discovered what seems to be materialism in the world today as part of his teachings. It is the same as saying this was the great enlightenment where he taught, "When we die, that's the end."

Certainly, the work of hospitals will end when people die. After people die, the funeral director will take over. They will take the body to be prayed for at a temple, cremated at the crematorium, and buried. This is the usual procedure. But this level of awareness is not very different from any ordinary people.

In the ancient past or medieval times in Japan, the people approved of the existence of souls, and so did people outside of Japan, such as China and India. They believed in them even though they were not visible to the eyes.

As for people today, because they cannot see, understand, and sense souls, denying their existence has become the norm. Can we say that this is because people have attained enlightenment from having lived in the modern civilization that has become advanced? Absolutely not. It just means they have become less able to see and understand spiritual matters.

With material abundance, many things have become convenient. As a consequence, if people are too absorbed in them, they will not be able to sense and understand spiritual things. Moreover, it will make them forget the importance of cultivating their senses and understanding the mind.

2

Curses Are Prevalent Even Today

Cursing was a criminal offense in the Heian period

For example, during the Heian period (9th to 12th century) in Japan, vengeful spirits were commonly believed by the majority of the people. My wife, who is currently researching curses of vengeful spirits, told me about something she read. One book said that at the beginning of the Heian period, cursing others to death was a criminal offense. If people killed another person through a curse, they would be executed, while attempted murder would put them in prison.

This means that they believed in the reality of curses and that is why there was a prison sentence.

The Bible says that Jesus Christ taught, "What you think in your mind can also be a sin." Jurists today are finding it hard to understand this concept, but people around the area of Palestine and Jerusalem believed in it. In addition, Japan in the Heian period had laws enacted upon it.

It means that when people curse another person, that itself is an action. "Thoughts equal action," the principle that works in the other world, also works in this world. So, those who try to harm others with their evil thoughts are actually committing a crime.

People in the Heian period actually died from getting cursed. They died from becoming ill or going insane, or they had a miscarriage or lost their child at a young age. Many things happened. Back then, people knew that these things were often due to the curses their rivals or enemies sent to them.

The so-called yin-yang masters were people working at the yin-yang office as a bureau or, in today's terms, governmental officials. These officially chosen yin-yang masters were public servants with supernatural powers. One of their main jobs was to protect the high-ranking governmental people and the important individuals in the imperial house, including their wives and children.

A samurai can protect such people from those who come attacking with a sword, but a yin-yang master was hired to protect them from anyone who would try to kill them or make them ill with their spiritual powers because they knew that it was real.

This leads me to mention that there were also many people with the powers of a yin-yang master who were not in any governmental position and only worked privately. These people were hired by individuals who were wronged and said, "We became bankrupt, banished, and poor because those in power are just doing what they want." Such people would hire these private yin-yang masters to put a deadly curse on them instead.

Aside from these people, there were official yin-yang masters. They were the Kamo clan such as Kamo-no-Yasunori and Mitsuyoshi, and also Abe-no-Seimei. They were trained people who would go out to search for the cause of any abnormality that made them think, "There must be a reason behind this." Once they discovered where the curse had come from, these people would conduct a special rite to repel it. In most cases, the cursed individuals are possessed, so these yin-yang masters would proactively try to exorcise it by removing what is possessing the person and expelling the cause related to the cursing.

Like so, there were times when people could actually sense these spiritual phenomena in the past. This was only a thousand years ago, but strangely, people today have gradually become less sensitive toward it.

Spiritual matters got pushed out from the subject of research and became unorthodox

In the West, it was after Descartes that people began acknowledging the soul and the physical body as separate entities. Descartes had the ability to sense spiritual matters, but he decided to focus his research only on worldly matters because he thought that ordinary people would not understand spiritual matters.

Then, after Kant, who lived around the Edo Period in Japan, the separation became more clear. Kant did not deny the other world or spiritual matters, but for his studies, he decided to focus only on issues that can be researched in a worldly sense. As a result, academics began to shift their focus to worldly issues only.

In other words, this is phenomenology. Research began to focus on worldly matters only simply because they couldn't find answers by researching spiritual matters. But those matters gradually got pushed out from the subject of research, and today, people have come to say that merely thinking about spiritual things is unorthodox.

Even by watching the exorcism-related movies made in places such as the U.S. or Europe, you will notice that more movies now depict the passive attitude of the Vatican.

The Vatican would expect the patients to first get checked up at the hospital and be hospitalized if a diagnosis can be found, and that they will conduct an exorcism on the patients only when the doctors clearly diagnose them to be untreatable at the hospital.

This is a very negative and pessimistic way of thinking that narrows down their work as a religious organization. But such exorcism-related cases are in fact prevalent in today's world.

People's thoughts are flying around and influencing each other. It is just like products such as television, radio, or mobile phones such as smartphones; they can pick up signals because they have an inbuilt device to receive them. Like so, the human body has a receiver that can pick up what other people send out.

I, like the Tokyo Tower or the second tower, Skytree, can pick up the thoughts of people all over Japan and the world. This is how I conduct spiritual messages.

This receiving ability of people nowadays has become weaker, or people forget that they have such an ability within them. Regardless, people are unconsciously influenced by various things they are receiving. This is the reality.

3

The Reason Shakyamuni Taught "Abandon Your Attachment"

Why Shakyamuni can be said to be the "Greatest Sorcerer"

Going back to the beginning, Shakyamuni Buddha taught the teachings on *muga* or "no self." Why so? This is because it was not desirable for humans to live selfishly. I believe I should elaborate on this, so I will talk more about it.

When humans are born, they first need to grow up physically, and during that period, becoming an adult is their main task. Humans would stop growing once they become the size of an adult, but until they do, growing up is most important to them. It may depend on each person's genetic blueprint, but for people to grow into adult size, they will need to eat, exercise, and study so that their brains develop. In the process, all the studying and exercising as well as living among many people—and practicing to take on various roles as if doing a role-play—are what humans go through to grow up. This is something that most people will need to experience.

Pandas, too, are only born weighing 100 plus grams, but within one year and a half to two years, they grow to their full size. In the case of wild pandas, that is when they depart from their parents and set off on their own into the woods. They would travel tens of kilometers and find their habitat in the mountains. They would find a mountain they could live in and survive on their own. If they don't, the parent and child will end up fighting with one another over food and have conflicts, so once the child turns into an adult, they part ways.

In this way, until human beings grow to their full size, they need to eat, sleep, and protect themselves. They will grow up feeling the importance of "food, sex, and sleep." Eating will be most important; especially for animals, this will be the top priority. Aside from that, because living beings are separated into males and females, such a divide invites interest in the opposite sex as humans grow up.

In terms of sleep, there are individual differences, so I cannot be certain, but people back in the day probably didn't think that it was so important.

In today's case, however, while you live, you will be living in this very materialistic world. So, if you do not sleep, you will not be able to interact with the spiritual world. A dream is often interpreted as a world that only appears in a dream, but in reality, a dream is often a time spent interacting with the Spirit World. Therefore, even today, people can be said to be spending a third of their life in the Spirit World while they sleep. In the past though, I believe people were more susceptible to spiritual influence even when they were awake.

Although people may wonder what Shakyamuni tried to teach, when you carefully consider his teachings, you may notice this: the teachings contain many things that you should actually say to the devils or lost spirits possessing the living when you exorcise, repel, or return them to heaven.

In other words, there's no problem if people die and return to the other world. However, if people have not only become a ghost wandering around in this world without returning to heaven, but have also become an evil being who is possessing and bringing suffering to living people and dragging them into hell, Buddhism is full of teachings to stop such evil actions.

Many scholars think that Shakyamuni's teachings are materialistic and philosophical, but quite the contrary, he was actually one of the greatest sorcerers or psychics. You will understand that this is quite true. Without such powers, he wouldn't have been able to teach what he did.

There are the teachings of *the impermanence of all things*, *the egolessness of all phenomena*, and *the perfect tranquility of nirvana*. They deny that existences in this world are eternal and absolute and teach the following: There is nothing eternal in this world. This world is a temporary and transient world, so if you have attachments to things of this world or attachments to your physical body, then you must abandon such a mindset.

For example, no matter how many treasures you have, you cannot take them with you to the other world. None of them are permanent in this world. No matter how great of a palace you build, you cannot take it back with you to the other world.

Therefore, you must not become attached to anything in this world.

The wisdom to overcome sufferings from the opposite sex

Food is usually the first thing to which people have attachments.

Attachment to food probably grows as food is a basic necessity to live in this world, and I believe people from ancient times practiced fasting to lessen their attachment to food as much as possible. They probably did so to overcome their instinctive nature and to find their spiritual self.

In this sense, we can understand the purpose of fasting, but everyone has to eat a certain amount to survive in this world; we have no choice. However, if we focus too much on eating, in other words, if we only eat gourmet food or eat excessively, then we would regard this world as heaven.

In terms of feelings toward the opposite sex, it can be beautiful if they are sublimated into poetries, novels, or music, but if instead people turn too animalistic, then in reality, they will become reckless and the strong will only take from the weak.

If we liken this to lions, one male will have many females. Under the protection of the strong male, the females would go hunting and take care of their offspring. A male that has many females by their side would have defeated many weak males and warded them off. According to the laws of nature, the weak will lose, and based on the survival of the fittest, the DNA of the ones with the greatest survival instinct will survive. If the DNA of the weak ones are preserved, then their species will become extinct, so naturally, the DNA of the stronger ones will be preserved and drive out the weak. This is what happens.

If we take a look at human society today, there are various "selling points," such as physical appearance, family background, fortune, and educational background. This applies to both males and females. Everyone tends to be overambitious to try to get what other people cannot get.

However, there will be problems if people greedily seek for more than what they deserve. When you seek more than what you deserve, then you may experience setbacks or suffering. Even if it seems like you have succeeded in this world, if the success exceeds the limit that you deserve, then that can cause problems or suffering, even with issues related to the opposite sex.

If both can support each other, and the relationship is in good condition for both to live through life together, then you will be forgiven to some extent. But in principle, issues to do with the opposite sex can often hinder your spiritual path. This is something you should know.

In Japanese, the kanji character for the word disturbance (*samatageru*)（妨）includes the radical for "women"（女）. This may sound sexist to females, but according to the history of Buddhism or other religions, the problems between the opposite sex can significantly affect humans, especially males. Females are usually the ones that cause a distraction to a male and vice versa; to a female, males could actually be their distraction.

Historically speaking, working female is still a new concept, and there aren't many types of work for them. So that is probably why it affects males more. But as for nuns, their distraction would be males in many cases.

As for males, when they want to master their way, for example, as a religious leader or as a swordsman and refine their sword skills, it would be very hard if they had a wife and children. There will be worldly restrictions that will disturb them from mastering the way. Of course, those with big ambitions will experience many other kinds of distractions also. This is the suffering that you will experience throughout your life, starting from youth.

Nowadays, more and more people are living their lives without getting married, and I can kind of understand why. It allows people to focus wholeheartedly on the self, and females who wish to work throughout their lives can do so without having to cater to another living person.

This is where difficult problems lie in how the future society should be.

In principle, it is already difficult to control your selfishness by yourself, but if you have a counterpart who becomes your partner, the worst-case scenario is that they will cause trouble, restrict, immobilize both of you, and neither of you would be able to do your work. And to overcome this situation, you would need a tremendous amount of insight from the power of wisdom.

In terms of Shakyamuni's wisdom, that is to know that everything is impermanent and every situation will pass by, like the flow of the river, so it is important to live simply and carefree.

Everything has a meeting and a separation. We can have feelings of attraction and love, as well as feelings of hatred and neglect. Many things happen in life, but it is essential not to get too caught up in them and just live your life without being too affected. This is Shakyamuni's way of thinking.

4

Be Ready to Return
to the Other World One Day

What you should know
in order not to become a lost spirit

The third seal of the Dharma is the perfect tranquility of nirvana.

> The world of nirvana is a tranquil place
> That exists after death.
> This teaches you that in the end,
> This world is a temporary world.
> In other words, you may have
> A physical body, food, a home, and
> Things that you could physically touch but
> This world is a transient world.
> When you return to the other world,
> You will not be able to touch the things of this world.
> What surprises people the most when they die is that
> After they die,
> They will go through the walls of their house and

92

Even if they say things,

The people on earth will not be able to hear them.

Excluding a few psychics, most people cannot

Hear their voice or see them.

They have no influence on the people of this world.

Even if they try to shake hands,

They cannot grasp their hands and

If they try to hug them, they will just pass through.

They enter a world like this.

This kind of world is not an abnormal world

But the true world.

People must be enlightened that the world where

They cannot touch material objects or things is in fact

The true world.

This is one of the crucial points to know when people move onto the Spirit World after they die and go to the heavenly world. Those who cannot awaken to this point are people who are living while restrained by worldly things. After death, those who think that they cannot go on without worldly things will not notice that they have died and will live in both worlds. However, even if they try talking to people, they are not heard and when they try to touch things, they cannot. They know that something strange is happening, but they cannot understand why and remain in this state. In most cases, these are what we call "lost spirits" that are wandering on earth.

Most of the time, all they can do is seek salvation from their family, relatives, friends, or coworkers but even if they approach them and try to cause some kind of physical phenomenon, they are unable to do so and are at a loss for what to do next. What they can do at most is to appear in the person's dream. If they are lucky enough, they may be able to create a spiritual phenomenon and the person can feel as if they were given a hint or hunch about something.

During times of war, mothers who remained in Japan and whose sons were off to the battlefield often had dreams of their sons coming back. In most cases, their son died during combat and their soul came back and appeared in the mother's dream. Things like this occurred.

It may be easy to understand if they were able to cause a phenomenon, much like a poltergeist, that people can physically sense but not everyone can do so. What they could do at most is to appear in the dreams of those they strongly loved such as their wife or mother.

When people are sleeping, they may have an out-of-body experience with the silver cord attached to their body. The part coming out of their physical body is similar to the state of a ghost so when they meet the deceased person, they are able to recognize that person.

In most cases, when people wake up, they usually forget about it so if they are not trained, they cannot remember who they have met in their dreams. However, I am sure that they remember things that left a strong impact on their minds when they were dreaming. So, mothers may remember dreaming about their sons coming home. That kind of thing can happen.

Of course, some spirits have the ability to cause various physical phenomena. It is hard to distinguish between those who can cause these things and those who cannot, but some spirits can make some kind of phenomena happen. For example, an object could drop suddenly, a lightbulb could go out, a candle could blow out, or a wind bell could ring. In regards to temples, there are many monks who have said that they heard the bell, the one they use when chanting the "Amitabha Buddha," ring. They hear it ring at midnight and will know that there will be a funeral the next day.

There is even a case where a blind person, much like *Hoichi the Earless*, heard the marching steps of the soldiers wearing their armor. The soldiers are the ghosts of the people written in *The Tales of the Heike*.

How these things materialize tends to vary based on the individual's ability. Since it depends on the spiritual ability of the person alive or the ability of the deceased person, I believe it is difficult to make a formula, at this time, based on what situations will cause a certain phenomenon. Additionally, I believe that there is a difference when the phenomenon is caused by the support of other spirits or without it.

A curious event that happened at the time one of my relatives passed away

One story I heard of that is related to this topic is a story of when my paternal grandmother passed away. My grandmother used to babysit my brother who was four years older than me, but when I was born, she said that she did not want to take care of another baby so she left for Tokyo to live with my uncle.

When my grandmother passed away, I lived in a house that was not so modern and had a wooden sliding door. When my father, mother, and aunt who was a writer, were talking in the living room, the sliding door opened about one foot. They were taken by great surprise because it was a sliding door, and so it could only be opened by a person. It cannot be opened by the wind so they went to see what opened it, but no one was there. Everyone said it was strange, but soon after, they heard the news that my grandmother had passed away.

Even in Master's Holy Temple, where I live, extraordinary things sometimes occur. When the father of my former wife, who was over the age of 70, fainted in the snow and was in grave condition, our elevator stopped. I believe it was past 4 p.m., but this unusual event where the elevator stopped made me wonder what had happened, and that was when he fainted. That is why I wonder what influences spiritual phenomena to occur.

From my own experiences, something similar happened when my brother passed away. I had trouble sleeping that night and I woke up around midnight or near daybreak. At that time, I lived in an apartment at Ikedayama and when I went to the bathroom and looked at the digital clock, it showed 4:44 a.m. The number 444 was shown on the digital display like a neon sign. I thought, "Oh wow! What an unpleasant number,[1] I wonder if something had happened," and I would later know that my brother passed away around that time. On that day, my brother's spirit came to Tokyo at noon and I spoke to him spiritually. I am unable to come up with a formula at this time stating how much of something could give a spiritual influence, but I can say that these types of things have occurred several times.

"Can you abandon all your attachments and leave this world?"

These things happen and in terms of Buddhist teachings —although Buddhist scholars will not understand this —what you need to say to lost spirits is to abandon any attachments they had when they lived as a human in this world. This is the royal road to save them.

I believe most of you may have some kind of attachment. For example, you may have attachments thinking things like "I want to eat food," "I want to drink juice" or "I want to drink alcohol." In addition, you may have attachments to your clothing, room, house, or the fact that you have graduated from a prestigious school, or are working at a renowned company. You have attachments regarding your friends and you may have various worries created by comparing yourself with others.

However, I must say to you; those things are all associated with this world. It is true that all of you live in such a situation but even if you live like that, you must be able to look at yourself objectively as if you are looking down at yourself from a distance. You must be prepared to answer the following question: "In the future, you must leave this world and you must abandon your attachments. When that happens, will you be able to leave this world without any problems?"

Some may say, "I am not ready to leave this world. I am worried about my child," or "I am worried about my husband," or "I am worried about my wife." There may be some who say, "I am worried about my parents who need my care," or "I am worried about my brother who may be doing reckless things" and the list goes on.

This is only natural to humans and acceptable to a certain degree, but if it exceeds the limit then I must say they are just wasting their energy. The reason is that if, after death, they continue being attached to those things, they cannot let go of this world. They cannot let go of their home. They cannot let go of their company. They cannot let go of their school.

Ghost stories at schools are usually related to this. I believe that individuals who died at school had attachments so they continue to appear there as ghosts for 10 years or so. However, this is because they were not taught these things. If at school they had learned what would become of them after death and what is the essence of humans, they may not have stayed as ghosts in the school for 10 years haunting the students and teachers.

But they weren't taught about these things. I presume they weren't taught about them at home either. So, when they experience something painful, such as simply getting a zero on their exam or their boyfriend being snatched away by someone else, then they may want to commit suicide by jumping off the roof.

They believe that they can escape their sufferings by dying but even if the physical body dies, *what was inside* continues to live on. So, the *thing that continues to live on* will have no idea what to do next. The people, not knowing they are spiritual existences, end up thinking, "What? I should've died but it seems I am still alive," and try to commit suicide again and again.

Seeing that nothing changes, they become bored and start to possess their friends or other people and causing accidents and creating disturbances. Eventually, their friends will graduate but they will remain in school. When they find students who have experienced similar things, such as wanting to commit suicide due to heartbreak, they possess that person and cause trouble one after another.

That is why they must understand the existence of the soul. And they must understand that, in this world, as spiritual training or a way to confirm their progress or growth, people may succeed in various things or advance in their skills, or things may go as they planned. This is truly great for them, and we must acknowledge this, but when they become souls, if their success, progress, and growth in this world become an attachment and they cannot leave this world, then this is in itself, failure. You must know about this.

Buddhism teaches that people must leave this world, go onto the next world and must start a new life in the other world. So, we must always be ready for this as we live.

5

Abandon Your Ego through Self-Reflection and Return to Your True Self

The difference between ego *and* self, *seen in koi*

According to the teachings of Shakyamuni Buddha, people in their young adult years—a period of growth—desire to grow and that becomes *ego*, but they must break away from it. This state of having ego has a quality that separates the individual and the other person and makes him or her try to outdo others in a fierce win-or-lose battle. In order to become successful, such quality may be necessary for entrance exams, the entertainment industry, or other sectors.

However, if I were to explain it another way, it can look similar to when feeding *koi* (Japanese carp). Let's say that you own many koi and you go to the pond to feed them, then the koi swarm in and open their mouths at the surface of the water. They push their bodies forward to get as much food as possible and they topple over and push each other. This is what it would be like to be *full of ego*. They want to eat food and prioritize themselves; this is what it is like to have *ego*.

On the other hand, a koi swimming nonchalantly in the big pond alone is like the appearance of someone who is exploring the *self*, not the ego. Buddhism teaches that within ego, there are aspects that harm others or hinder an individual's spiritual growth through pursuing worldly success and progress or having pride, superiority toward others, or a false self. Those who live pursuing these things must cast away their wrong ways and must outgrow their ego. They must try to return to their original *self*. That is why Shakyamuni teaches us to abandon ego but not abandon the self. In other words, we must continue to seek and explore the self.

The self mentioned here is the original nature of the soul. It is important to continue exploring the good natures of the soul. But when you are living in this world and live with a physical body using your six sensory organs—the eyes, ears, nose, tongue, tactile body, and mind—and are swayed by worldly delusions that arise from your five senses, you start to believe that ego is you and forget your true self.

The importance of self-reflection as seen in the rice husk analogy

You must grasp the true self. You must explore your *true self*. The practices of Zen are mostly about this topic. They do meditation but for what? They undergo this training to regain their *true self* by self-reflection, removing the dust, dirt or shell that covered it while living with worldly desires.

In other words, it is like a grain of rice. In order to protect the rice, there is a husk. A husk surrounds it and it is crucial to have a husk to cover the rice. However, if the husk is still intact then it would be difficult to make the rice available to eat. The husk itself is made to protect the rice and in a way, it is like a layer of self-preservation but to a certain degree, this is necessary. However, if the rice were to be eaten and converted into energy, we must remove the husk and polish it. By doing so, it will then become food for people and be broken down into nutrients.

In order to become a more independent person, it is necessary to take care of yourself and to have responsibility for your growth, so in some meaning, it is OK to have a barrier or husk to protect yourself during growth. However, when you truly want to contribute to this world or to be of use to others, you must shed your husk. If you are not able to become white rice, you will not be able to contribute so you must cast off your shell.

In other words, if you continue to wear the husk, it would mean that you differentiate yourself from others and you are thinking only about how much more you can take. If the competition between you and the other person is for the sake of improving each other, it is OK. On the other hand, you have lived wrongly if you thought that "Worldly things ultimately decide who is superior, the ranking of a person and his or her success, and nothing else matters. Everything will end once you die so how much you can enjoy life now will amount to how much you loved yourself." In this case, you will have to reflect on your life.

However, there are those who cannot reflect even when they go to the other world. Self-reflection is another thing that is not taught at school. They do not teach you that you are a spiritual being and the essence of a human is the soul as well as the importance of self-reflection. Nowadays, they do not even teach enough on the topic of morality. While they are alive, they must reflect on their actions if they have said bad words or have done wrong things, hurt other people's feelings for self-centered reasons or if they lost loyalty inside a group.

Reflect over selfish actions and thoughts that cause harm or curses

In the end, what is ego? It is often said that the hearts of children are pure and they are able to see angels or the spirits of the other world. There are accounts like this but it is also true that during their childhood, their ego is already growing.

For example, if they walk past a store, they may say "I want that candy" or "I want that chocolate bar" and start to roll around on the ground and have a fit. This is a sign that their ego is already forming during their childhood. Such a character appears during adulthood in different forms that make them desire various things. The child continues to say that they want it no matter what and even if you say, "It is not time for that. We will have dinner in an hour so maybe next time," they may not listen to you. Even adults have this kind of behavior and sometimes it is said that during their final years of life, they start to become childish. It is often said that once people get older, they become selfish like a child. But it is necessary for you to have it under control.

It is important that what you are doing does not become something that is self-centered but you must also make sure that you are not having thoughts that may cause harm to others or may cause a curse or a spell. This will, without a doubt, be recorded in your soul. If you look at it from the laws that govern all living things, the kind of evil thoughts that try to curse or bring a person harm will come back to you and will hinder your progress. It will draw you into the world of darkness and in the end, you will lose friends and the future that awaits you will be one where you will live alone in a deep well or cave in the Spirit World. That is why I would like you to refrain from becoming such a person.

Although you may try to make it look good on the surface, people around you will notice that you have a selfish mind and you will be isolated, and your friendship or romantic relationship will not last. This is the reason why you should know about these things.

Even if you do self-reflection, you cannot see it, others may not recognize it, and even you, yourself may not know whether it is working or not. But you must think and reflect on your day's thoughts and actions one by one as if you are peeling the rice husk one by one.

When you reflect, you may have thoughts such as, "My thoughts in the morning were bad," "the phone call that I made might have hurt the other person's feelings" or "I had plans to do work but I slacked off putting my personal matters first" or "I should have helped the other person but because I wanted to cause her trouble, I didn't." In short, I would like for you to be careful because self-prioritizing ways of living will increase your ego even more.

6

Tengu or Youma That Is Born from Expanding Your Ego

If you focus only on expanding your ego, you will become the so-called tengu-type person. Tengu is an existence that loves climbing up the slope and getting to the top. In picture books, they tend to have wings and their nose up in the air. It means they have a boasting heart. Their nose is stuck up high, and they wear an *eboshi* (a hat worn by Japanese aristocrats) and a Japanese single tooth *geta* (clog), and they walk up the slope. They are able to walk up the steps but cannot climb down because they will tumble over.

In short, tengu-type people can live happily when they are *going up* and receiving praise from those around them. However, when everything seems to be *going down*, they can only fall into despair and they continue this cycle. I believe it is wise for you not to become like this.

Tengu has wings, so you may think of them as angels but generally, they are a type of youkai, so you can think of them as the beginnings of youkai and the fallen ones on the path to evil. They wish for their success and think only about going up; there are many people like this in this era. People exceeding in various areas, such as in a prestigious school, a famous company or a place where sales competition is cut-throat, may be considered "winners" in a worldly context. Still, most of the time, these people are tengu when viewed spiritually.

They do not have a heart of mercy or the heart of love toward others and do not have the heart to reflect on themselves and continue going after their own success. That is why they become tengu when they die. Their nose is long because they only boast about themselves and they can only think about going up and using their leaf, a Japanese aralia, to make a gust of wind to power through. I believe there are people with this kind of attitude toward life.

This is one of the paths to evil so if they think that they are on this path, they must reflect on it a little and become more human-like. They must know more about love and self-reflection. They must abandon their attachment to this world and must reconsider their way of thinking which is based solely on the hierarchical relationship between people.

In addition to tengu, there is something called *youma* and it exists in Japan and China. In English, it means demon and these creatures have mysterious powers. They use their sexiness and show people a flamboyant world to lure them in.

If you go to Ginza, there are various bar businesses such as luxurious clubs and many of them are influenced by the power of *inari* (fox deity)—although not to the level of a nine-tail fox—and they make a flamboyant world and trick people to get money out of them. Indeed, this is one of the worlds of youma. To phrase it mildly, it can lead to the world of youkai, but if this goes further onto the wrong path, it will lead to a world of devils. There are many people who try to gain money, fame, or power through sex appeal or looks but they must know that although it may look like success, it is actually a way to hell.

In the drama, *Kurokawa no Techou* (lit. "Black Leather Notebook"), the actress Emi Takei had a role as the cunning woman, and the original novel and drama were entertaining but the kind of mindset of this character will lead you to hell. The main character became youma and swindled money with her looks, and she repeatedly tricked them. It seems that she may gain influence in this world and compete to become the number one hostess in Ginza, but what awaits her in most cases is destruction and catastrophe. After she dies, she will become a lost ghost and she will once again become a youkai-like existence that will make people go astray. In some cases, she may just become a demon right off the bat.

That is why, instead of amplifying those kinds of evil desires or getting caught up in achieving success in a short period of time, you should have a sacred mind and continue to make diligent efforts. Although you may have made efforts and achieved results, you must not think of the results as your own but as belonging to all the people and it is important to have a heart of wanting to serve the public.

In this chapter, I talked about "Ego, Self, and Self-Reflection." In Buddhism, this is the basics of the basics and if you are able to at least master the topics covered in this lecture, then much fewer people will wander as ghosts after death.

You will not understand this content easily just by having modern education and experience. I believe that if you do not have the heart to learn more and study the Truth more, it will not be easy for you. However, if you were to understand at least the content of this chapter, then I believe you will not have to wander as ghosts.

TRANSLATOR'S NOTE

1 The number 4, pronounced *shi* in Japanese, has the same pronunciation as *shi* or death and is traditionally considered an unlucky number in some Asian countries.

Afterword

How you control yourself from cursing others and how you prevent yourself from getting cursed; these are both one aspect of life training, and although easy, one aspect of enlightenment, too.

The law of cause and effect is at work in this world.

Those who love others will be loved, and those who curse others will be disliked.

What this book tells you is not very difficult.

When you want to curse someone, congratulate that person.

When you want to take love from someone, give love to that person.

Those who envy people are unhappy people.

Now is the time to study the teachings of egolessness and emptiness, and have the mind to be content.

Calmly ward off jealousy and endeavor to become a useful person to society. It will help you avoid becoming a lost spirit in hell and having to suffer a few hundred years there.

Ryuho Okawa
Master & CEO of Happy Science Group
August 23, 2022

For a deeper understanding of
The Spiritual Truth About Curses and Spells
see the book below by Ryuho Okawa:

The Laws of the Sun [New York: IRH Press, 2018]

ABOUT THE AUTHOR

Founder and CEO of Happy Science Group.

Ryuho Okawa was born on July 7th 1956, in Tokushima, Japan. After graduating from the University of Tokyo with a law degree, he joined a Tokyo-based trading house. While working at its New York headquarters, he studied international finance at the Graduate Center of the City University of New York. In 1981, he attained Great Enlightenment and became aware that he is El Cantare with a mission to bring salvation to all humankind.

In 1986, he established Happy Science. It now has members in over 165 countries across the world, with more than 700 branches and temples as well as 10,000 missionary houses around the world.

He has given over 3,450 lectures (of which more than 150 are in English) and published over 3,050 books (of which more than 600 are Spiritual Interview Series), and many are translated into 40 languages. Along with *The Laws of the Sun* and *The Laws Of Messiah*, many of the books have become best sellers or million sellers. To date, Happy Science has produced 25 movies. The original story and original concept were given by the Executive Producer Ryuho Okawa. He has also composed music and written lyrics of over 450 pieces.

Moreover, he is the Founder of Happy Science University and Happy Science Academy (Junior and Senior High School), Founder and President of the Happiness Realization Party, Founder and Honorary Headmaster of Happy Science Institute of Government and Management, Founder of IRH Press Co., Ltd., and the Chairperson of NEW STAR PRODUCTION Co., Ltd. and ARI Production Co., Ltd.

WHAT IS EL CANTARE?

El Cantare means "the Light of the Earth," and is the Supreme God of the Earth who has been guiding humankind since the beginning of Genesis. He is whom Jesus called Father and Muhammad called Allah, and is *Ame-no-Mioya-Gami*, Japanese Father God. Different parts of El Cantare's core consciousness have descended to Earth in the past, once as Alpha and another as Elohim. His branch spirits, such as Shakyamuni Buddha and Hermes, have descended to Earth many times and helped to flourish many civilizations. To unite various religions and to integrate various fields of study in order to build a new civilization on Earth, a part of the core consciousness has descended to Earth as Master Ryuho Okawa.

Alpha is a part of the core consciousness of El Cantare who descended to Earth around 330 million years ago. Alpha preached Earth's Truths to harmonize and unify Earth-born humans and space people who came from other planets.

Elohim is a part of El Cantare's core consciousness who descended to Earth around 150 million years ago. He gave wisdom, mainly on the differences of light and darkness, good and evil.

Ame-no-Mioya-Gami (Japanese Father God) is the Creator God and the Father God who appears in the ancient literature, *Hotsuma Tsutae*. It is believed that He descended on the foothills of Mt. Fuji about 30,000 years ago and built the Fuji dynasty, which is the root of the Japanese civilization. With justice as the central pillar, Ame-no-Mioya-Gami's teachings spread to ancient civilizations of other countries in the world.

Shakyamuni Buddha was born as a prince into the Shakya Clan in India around 2,600 years ago. When he was 29 years old, he renounced the world and sought enlightenment. He later attained Great Enlightenment and founded Buddhism.

Hermes is one of the 12 Olympian gods in Greek mythology, but the spiritual Truth is that he taught the teachings of love and progress around 4,300 years ago that became the origin of the current Western civilization. He is a hero that truly existed.

Ophealis was born in Greece around 6,500 years ago and was the leader who took an expedition to as far as Egypt. He is the God of miracles, prosperity, and arts, and is known as Osiris in the Egyptian mythology.

Rient Arl Croud was born as a king of the ancient Incan Empire around 7,000 years ago and taught about the mysteries of the mind. In the heavenly world, he is responsible for the interactions that take place between various planets.

Thoth was an almighty leader who built the golden age of the Atlantic civilization around 12,000 years ago. In the Egyptian mythology, he is known as god Thoth.

Ra Mu was a leader who built the golden age of the civilization of Mu around 17,000 years ago. As a religious leader and a politician, he ruled by uniting religion and politics.

A New Genre of Spiritual Mystery Novels
- The Unknown Stigma Trilogy -

Coming on October 1, 2022

The Unknown Stigma 1
<The Mystery>

Hardcover • 192 pages • $17.95
ISBN: 978-1-942125-28-0

The first spiritual mystery novel by Ryuho Okawa. It happened
one early summer afternoon, in a densely wooded park in Tokyo:
following a loud scream of a young woman, the alleged victim
was found lying with his eyes rolled back and foaming at the
mouth. But there was no sign of forced trauma, nor even a drop
of blood. Then, similar murder cases continued one after another
without any clues. Later, this mysterious serial murder case leads
back to a young Catholic nun...

Coming in November 2022

The Unknown Stigma 2
<The Resurrection>

Hardcover • 180 pages • $17.95
ISBN: 978-1-942125-31-0

A sequel to *The Unknown Stigma 1 <The Mystery>* by Ryuho Okawa. After an extraordinary spiritual experience, a young, mysterious Catholic nun is now endowed with a new, noble mission. What kind of destiny will she face? Will it be hope or despair that awaits her? The story develops into a turn of events that no one could ever have anticipated. Are you ready to embrace its shocking ending?

Coming in December 2022

The Unknown Stigma 3
<The Universe>

Hardcover • 184 pages • $17.95
ISBN: 978-1-958655-00-9

In this astonishing sequel to the first two installments of *The Unknown Stigma*, the protagonist journeys through the universe and encounters a mystical world unknown to humankind. Discover what awaits her beyond this mysterious world.

RELATED BOOKS

THE REAL EXORCIST

ATTAIN WISDOM TO CONQUER EVIL

Paperback • 208 pages • $16.95
ISBN:978-1-942125-67-9 (Jun. 15, 2020)

This is a profound spiritual text backed by the author's nearly 40 years of real-life experience with spiritual phenomena. In it, Okawa teaches how we may discern and overcome our negative tendencies, by acquiring the right knowledge, mindset and lifestyle.

THE HELL YOU NEVER KNEW

AND HOW TO AVOID GOING THERE

Paperback • 192 pages • $15.95
ISBN: 978-1-942125-52-5 (Jul. 15, 2019)

From ancient times, people have been warned of the danger of falling to Hell. But does the world of Hell truly exist? If it does, what kind of people would go there? Through his spiritual abilities, Ryuho Okawa found out that Hell is only a small part of the vast Spirit World, yet more than half of the people today go there after they die.

THE MYSTICAL LAWS

GOING BEYOND THE DIMENSIONAL BOUNDARIES

Paperback • 250 pages • $14.95
ISBN: 978-1-941779-48-4 (Mar. 5, 2015)

"I believe that once you have finished reading this book, you will find it impossible to return to your old self, for you have now learned the secrets that run through this world and the other.

When you have learned of what has been hidden, will you feel guilt or will you find courage welling up from within?"

-From the Afterword

Published on August 15, 2022

THE REBIRTH OF BUDDHA

MY ETERNAL DISCIPLES,
HEAR MY WORDS

Paperback • 280 pages • $17.95
ISBN: 978-1-942125-95-2

These are the messages of Buddha who has returned to this modern age as promised to His eternal beloved disciples. They are in simple words and poetic style, yet contain profound messages. Once you start reading these passages, your soul will be replenished as the plant absorbs the water, and you will remember why you chose this era to be born into with Buddha. Listen to the voices of your Eternal Master and awaken to your calling.

Published on June 15, 2022

DEVELOPMENTAL STAGES OF LOVE - THE ORIGINAL THEORY

PHILOSOPHY OF LOVE IN MY YOUTH

Hardcover • 200 pages • $17.95
ISBN: 978-1-942125-94-5

This book is about author Ryuho Okawa's original philosophy of love which serves as the foundation of love in the chapter three of *The Laws of the Sun*. It consists of series of short essays authored during his age of 25 through 28 while he was working as a young promising business elite at an international trading company after attaining the Great Enlightenment in 1981. The developmental stages of love unites love and enlightenment, West and East, and bridges Christianity and Buddhism.

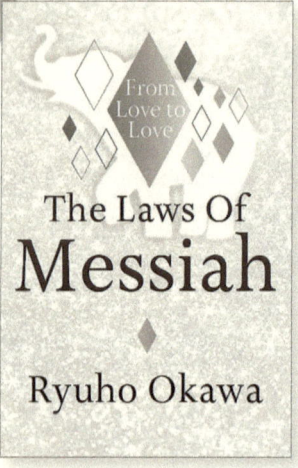

The Laws Of
Messiah

Ryuho Okawa

The Laws Of Messiah
From Love to Love

Paperback • 248 pages • $16.95
ISBN: 978-1-942125-90-7 (Jan. 31, 2022)

"What is Messiah?" This book carries an important message of love and guidance to people living now from the Modern-Day Messiah or the Modern-Day Savior. It also reveals the secret of Shambhala, the spiritual center of Earth, as well as the truth that this spiritual center is currently in danger of perishing and what we can do to protect this sacred place.

Love your Lord God. Know that those who don't know love don't know God. Discover the true love of God and the ideal practice of faith. This book teaches the most important element we must not lose sight of as we go through our soul training on this planet Earth.

THE ESSENCE OF BUDDHA

THE PATH TO ENLIGHTENMENT

Paperback • 208 pages • $14.95
ISBN: 978-1-942125-06-8 (Oct.1, 2016)

In this book, Ryuho Okawa imparts in simple and accessible language his wisdom about the essence of Shakyamuni Buddha's philosophy of life and enlightenment-teachings that have been inspiring people all over the world for over 2,500 years. By offering a new perspective on core Buddhist thoughts that have long been cloaked in mystique, Okawa brings these teachings to life for modern people. *The Essence of Buddha* distills a way of life that anyone can practice to achieve a life of self-growth, compassionate living, and true happiness.

THE TRILOGY

The Laws Series is an annual volume of books that are comprised of Ryuho Okawa's lectures that function as universal guidance to all people. They are of various topics that were given in accordance with the changes that each year brings. *The Laws of the Sun*, the first publication of the laws series, ranked in the annual best-selling list in Japan in 1994. Since, the laws series' titles have ranked in the annual best-selling list every year for more than two decades, setting socio-cultural trends in Japan and around the world.

THE LAWS OF THE SUN

ONE SOURCE, ONE PLANET, ONE PEOPLE

Paperback • 288 pages • $15.95
ISBN: 978-1-942125-43-3 (Oct. 15, 2018)

IMAGINE IF YOU COULD ASK GOD why He created this world and what spiritual laws He used to shape us— and everything around us. If we could understand His designs and intentions, we could discover what our goals in life should be and whether our actions move us closer to those goals or farther away.

At a young age, a spiritual calling prompted Ryuho Okawa to outline what he innately understood to be universal truths for all humankind. In *The Laws of the Sun*, Okawa outlines these laws of the universe and provides a road map for living one's life with greater purpose and meaning. In this powerful book, Ryuho Okawa reveals the transcendent nature of consciousness and the secrets of our multidimensional universe and our place in it. By understanding the different stages of love and following the Buddhist Eightfold Path, he believes we can speed up our eternal process of development. *The Laws of the Sun* shows the way to realize true happiness—a happiness that continues from this world through the other.

THE GOLDEN LAWS

HISTORY THROUGH THE EYES OF THE ETERNAL BUDDHA

E-book • 201 pages • $13.99
ISBN: 978-1-941779-82-8 (Jul. 1, 2011)

Throughout history, Great Guiding Spirits have been present on Earth in both the East and the West at crucial points in human history to further our spiritual development. *The Golden Laws* reveals how Divine Plan has been unfolding on Earth, and outlines 5,000 years of the secret history of humankind. Once we understand the true course of history, through past, present and into the future, we cannot help but become aware of the significance of our spiritual mission in the present age.

THE NINE DIMENSIONS

UNVEILING THE LAWS OF ETERNITY

Paperback • 168 pages • $15.95
ISBN: 978-0-982698-56-3 (Feb. 16, 2012)

This book is a window into the mind of our loving God, who designed this world and the vast, wondrous world of our afterlife as a school with many levels through which our souls learn and grow. When the religions and cultures of the world discover the truth of their common spiritual origin, they will be inspired to accept their differences, come together under faith in God, and build an era of harmony and peaceful progress on Earth.

THE LAWS OF SECRET

AWAKEN TO THIS NEW WORLD AND CHANGE YOUR LIFE

Paperback • 248 pages • $16.95
ISBN: 978-1-942125-81-5 (Apr. 20, 2021)

Our physical world coexists with the multi-dimensional spirit world and we are constantly interacting with some kind of spiritual energy, whether positive or negative, without consciously realizing it. This book reveals how our lives are affected by invisible influences, including the spiritual reasons behind influenza, the novel coronavirus infection, and other illnesses. The new view of the world in this book will inspire you to change your life in a better direction, and to become someone who can give hope and courage to others in this age of confusion.

SECRETS OF THE EVERLASTING TRUTHS

A NEW PARADIGM FOR LIVING ON EARTH

Paperback • 144 pages • $14.95
ISBN: 978-1-937673-10-9 (Apr. 27, 2012)

Okawa offers a glimpse of the vast universe created by God and discloses that humanity is intimately guided by celestial influences. Our planet will experience a decisive paradigm shift of "knowledge" and "truth," culminating in an era of paradoxical spirituality, where mastery of science will depend on spiritual knowledge. The advancement that we seek, resides within us.

OTHER RECOMMENDED TITLES

THE LAWS OF FAITH
One World Beyond Differences

THE LAWS OF BRONZE
Love One Another, Become One People

THE TRUE EIGHTFOLD PATH
Guideposts for Self-innovation

THE POWER OF BASICS
Introduction to Modern Zen Life of
Calm, Spirituality and Success

BASICS OF EXORCISM
How to Protect You and Your Family from Evil Spirits

ROJIN, BUDDHA'S MYSTICAL POWER
Its Ultimate Attainment in Today's World

THE POSSESSION
Know the Ghost Condition and
Overcome Negative Spiritual Influence

HEALING FROM WITHIN
Life-Changing Keys to Calm, Spiritual, and Healthy Living

THE UNHAPPINESS SYNDROME
28 Habits of Unhappy People (and How to Change Them)

For a complete list of books, visit okawabooks.com

MUSIC BY RYUHO OKAWA

El Cantare Ryuho Okawa Original Songs

A song celebrating Lord God

A song celebrating Lord God,
the God of the Earth,
who is beyond a prophet.

DVD
CD

The Water Revolution

English and Chinese version

For the truth and happiness of
the 1.4 billion people in China
who have no freedom. Love,
justice, and sacred rage of God
are on this melody that will
give you courage to fight to
bring peace.

DVD

CD

Search on YouTube

 the water revolution   for a short ad!

Listen now today!

 Download from
Spotify **iTunes** **Amazon**

With Savior *English version*

This is the message of hope to the modern people who are living in the midst of the Coronavirus pandemic, natural disasters, economic depression, and other various crises.

Search on YouTube

with savior 🔍 for a short ad!

The Thunder
a composition for repelling the Coronavirus

We have been granted this music from our Lord. It will repel away the novel Coronavirus originated in China. Experience this magnificent powerful music.

Search on YouTube

the thunder composition 🔍

for a short ad!

The Exorcism
prayer music for repelling Lost Spirits

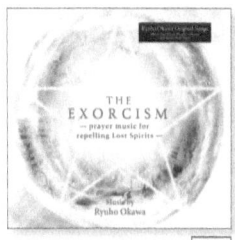

Feel the divine vibrations of this Japanese and Western exorcising symphony to banish all evil possessions you suffer from and to purify your space!

Search on YouTube

the exorcism repelling 🔍

for a short ad!

Listen now today!

 Download from
Spotify iTunes Amazon

DVD, CD available at amazon.com, and Happy Science locations worldwide

ABOUT HAPPY SCIENCE

Happy Science is a global movement that empowers individuals to find purpose and spiritual happiness and to share that happiness with their families, societies, and the world. With more than 12 million members around the world, Happy Science aims to increase awareness of spiritual truths and expand our capacity for love, compassion, and joy so that together we can create the kind of world we all wish to live in.

Activities at Happy Science are based on the Principle of Happiness (Love, Wisdom, Self-Reflection, and Progress). This principle embraces worldwide philosophies and beliefs, transcending boundaries of culture and religions.

Love teaches us to give ourselves freely without expecting anything in return; it encompasses giving, nurturing, and forgiving.

Wisdom leads us to the insights of spiritual truths, and opens us to the true meaning of life and the will of God (the universe, the highest power, Buddha).

Self-Reflection brings a mindful, nonjudgmental lens to our thoughts and actions to help us find our truest selves—the essence of our souls—and deepen our connection to the highest power. It helps us attain a clean and peaceful mind and leads us to the right life path.

Progress emphasizes the positive, dynamic aspects of our spiritual growth—actions we can take to manifest and spread happiness around the world. It's a path that not only expands our soul growth, but also furthers the collective potential of the world we live in.

PROGRAMS AND EVENTS

The doors of Happy Science are open to all. We offer a variety of programs and events, including self-exploration and self-growth programs, spiritual seminars, meditation and contemplation sessions, study groups, and book events.

Our programs are designed to:
* Deepen your understanding of your purpose and meaning in life
* Improve your relationships and increase your capacity to love unconditionally
* Attain peace of mind, decrease anxiety and stress, and feel positive
* Gain deeper insights and a broader perspective on the world
* Learn how to overcome life's challenges
   ... and much more.

For more information, visit <u>happy-science.org</u>.

CONTACT INFORMATION

Happy Science is a worldwide organization with branches and temples around the globe. For a comprehensive list, visit the worldwide directory at happy-science.org. The following are some of the many Happy Science locations:

UNITED STATES AND CANADA

New York
79 Franklin St., New York, NY 10013, USA
Phone: 1-212-343-7972
Fax: 1-212-343-7973
Email: ny@happy-science.org
Website: happyscience-usa.org

New Jersey
66 Hudson St., #2R, Hoboken, NJ 07030, USA
Phone: 1-201-313-0127
Email: nj@happy-science.org
Website: happyscience-usa.org

Chicago
2300 Barrington Rd., Suite #400,
Hoffman Estates, IL 60169, USA
Phone: 1-630-937-3077
Email: chicago@happy-science.org
Website: happyscience-usa.org

Florida
5208 8th St., Zephyrhills, FL 33542, USA
Phone: 1-813-715-0000
Fax: 1-813-715-0010
Email: florida@happy-science.org
Website: happyscience-usa.org

Atlanta
1874 Piedmont Ave., NE Suite 360-C
Atlanta, GA 30324, USA
Phone: 1-404-892-7770
Email: atlanta@happy-science.org
Website: happyscience-usa.org

San Francisco
525 Clinton St.
Redwood City, CA 94062, USA
Phone & Fax: 1-650-363-2777
Email: sf@happy-science.org
Website: happyscience-usa.org

Los Angeles
1590 E. Del Mar Blvd., Pasadena, CA
91106, USA
Phone: 1-626-395-7775
Fax: 1-626-395-7776
Email: la@happy-science.org
Website: happyscience-usa.org

Orange County
16541 Gothard St. Suite 104
Huntington Beach, CA 92647
Phone: 1-714-659-1501
Email: oc@happy-science.org
Website: happyscience-usa.org

San Diego
7841 Balboa Ave. Suite #202
San Diego, CA 92111, USA
Phone: 1-626-395-7775
Fax: 1-626-395-7776
E-mail: sandiego@happy-science.org
Website: happyscience-usa.org

Hawaii
Phone: 1-808-591-9772
Fax: 1-808-591-9776
Email: hi@happy-science.org
Website: happyscience-usa.org

Kauai
3343 Kanakolu Street, Suite 5
Lihue, HI 96766, USA
Phone: 1-808-822-7007
Fax: 1-808-822-6007
Email: kauai-hi@happy-science.org
Website: happyscience-usa.org

Toronto

845 The Queensway
Etobicoke, ON M8Z 1N6, Canada
Phone: 1-416-901-3747
Email: toronto@happy-science.org
Website: happy-science.ca

Vancouver

#201-2607 East 49th Avenue,
Vancouver, BC, V5S 1J9, Canada
Phone: 1-604-437-7735
Fax: 1-604-437-7764
Email: vancouver@happy-science.org
Website: happy-science.ca

INTERNATIONAL

Tokyo

1-6-7 Togoshi, Shinagawa,
Tokyo, 142-0041, Japan
Phone: 81-3-6384-5770
Fax: 81-3-6384-5776
Email: tokyo@happy-science.org
Website: happy-science.org

Seoul

74, Sadang-ro 27-gil,
Dongjak-gu, Seoul, Korea
Phone: 82-2-3478-8777
Fax: 82-2-3478-9777
Email: korea@happy-science.org
Website: happyscience-korea.org

London

3 Margaret St.
London, W1W 8RE United Kingdom
Phone: 44-20-7323-9255
Fax: 44-20-7323-9344
Email: eu@happy-science.org
Website: www.happyscience-uk.org

Taipei

No. 89, Lane 155, Dunhua N. Road,
Songshan District, Taipei City 105, Taiwan
Phone: 886-2-2719-9377
Fax: 886-2-2719-5570
Email: taiwan@happy-science.org
Website: happyscience-tw.org

Sydney

516 Pacific Highway, Lane Cove North,
2066 NSW, Australia
Phone: 61-2-9411-2877
Fax: 61-2-9411-2822
Email: sydney@happy-science.org

Kuala Lumpur

No 22A, Block 2, Jalil Link Jalan Jalil
Jaya 2, Bukit Jalil 57000,
Kuala Lumpur, Malaysia
Phone: 60-3-8998-7877
Fax: 60-3-8998-7977
Email: malaysia@happy-science.org
Website: happyscience.org.my

Sao Paulo

Rua. Domingos de Morais 1154,
Vila Mariana, Sao Paulo SP
CEP 04010-100, Brazil
Phone: 55-11-5088-3800
Email: sp@happy-science.org
Website: happyscience.com.br

Kathmandu

Kathmandu Metropolitan City,
Ward No. 15, Ring Road, Kimdol,
Sitapaila Kathmandu, Nepal
Phone: 977-1-427-2931
Email: nepal@happy-science.org

Jundiai

Rua Congo, 447, Jd. Bonfiglioli
Jundiai-CEP, 13207 340, Brazil
Phone: 55-11-4587-5952
Email: jundiai@happy-science.org

Kampala

Plot 877 Rubaga Road, Kampala
P.O. Box 34130 Kampala, UGANDA
Phone: 256-79-4682-121
Email: uganda@happy-science.org

HAPPY SCIENCE UNIVERSITY

THE FOUNDING SPIRIT AND THE GOAL OF EDUCATION

Based on the founding philosophy of the university, "Exploration of happiness and the creation of a new civilization," education, research and studies will be provided to help students acquire deep understanding grounded in religious belief and advanced expertise with the objectives of producing "great talents of virtue" who can contribute in a broad-ranging way to serve Japan and the international society.

FACULTIES

Faculty of human happiness

Students in this faculty will pursue liberal arts from various perspectives with a multidisciplinary approach, explore and envision an ideal state of human beings and society.

Faculty of successful management

This faculty aims to realize successful management that helps organizations to create value and wealth for society and to contribute to the happiness and the development of management and employees as well as society as a whole.

Faculty of future creation

Students in this faculty study subjects such as political science, journalism, performing arts and artistic expression, and explore and present new political and cultural models based on truth, goodness and beauty.

Faculty of future industry

This faculty aims to nurture engineers who can resolve various issues facing modern civilization from a technological standpoint and contribute to the creation of new industries of the future.

ABOUT HS PRESS

HS Press is an imprint of IRH Press Co., Ltd. IRH Press Co., Ltd., based in Tokyo, was founded in 1987 as a publishing division of Happy Science. IRH Press publishes religious and spiritual books, journals, magazines and also operates broadcast and film production enterprises. For more information, visit *okawabooks.com*.

Follow us on:

f Facebook: Okawa Books   **☉** Instagram: OkawaBooks
▶ Youtube: Okawa Books   **▼** Twitter: Okawa Books
℗ Pinterest: Okawa Books   **g** Goodreads: Ryuho Okawa

——— **NEWSLETTER** ———

To receive book related news, promotions and events, please subscribe to our newsletter below.

∞ eepurl.com/bsMeJj

 ——— **AUDIO / VISUAL MEDIA** ———

YOUTUBE   **PODCAST**

Introduction of Ryuho Okawa's titles; topics ranging from self-help, current affairs, spirituality, religion, and the universe.